CHURCH AND CONGREGATION:

A

PLEA FOR THEIR UNITY.

BY

C. A. BARTOL.

"For he is our peace, who hath made both one, and hath broken down the middle wall of partition between us." — EPHESIANS ii. 14.

BOSTON:
TICKNOR AND FIELDS.
M DCCC LVIII.

CAMBRIDGE:
METCALF AND COMPANY, PRINTERS TO THE UNIVERSITY.

CONTENTS.

CHURCH AND CONGREGATION.

INTRODUCTION.

THAT my aim at the outset may be fully understood, I must confess a motive for the composition of this book partly in the indirect relations of its subject. An inquiry as to the external form alone of the Church would have little attraction for my own mind. But every member of the community is vitally concerned in what a particular ecclesiastical constitution may morally imply. By no unmeaning chance is the Church so often on our tongues. Not in vain does the reformer with his sharpest criticisms pay to her his respects. No rotten and crumbling ark do her children stay up and bear on with their hands. What but the Church is rooted and growing for ever in the all-wasting floods of time? No other institution of government or society, from the farthest right to the extreme left of human speculation, so widely and closely touches the thought of the age. How many conflicts rage within and around these ancient walls! He that is disposed hastily to despise them as foolish strifes, must have adopted a philosophy of human nature very shallow, however transcendental it may be deemed. The world does not fight its battles for nothing. It would be just as sensible to speak contemptuously of Marathon, or Waterloo, or Bunker Hill, as of any of the past or present fiercer shocks when one idea encounters another. The soul repudiates the scorn. I must at least therefore assume my general topic to be not undeserving of regard.

The Congregational theory, however, of the Church, held by Congregationalists as I have known them, I have to say, is peculiar. I speak of that theory, not merely according to the sentence of any Cambridge or other platform, but with regard to its tacit assumptions and real concessions now. It admits the existence of two religious bodies in one, parted by a ritual line which is no real boundary; there being on either side persons to whom no true and liberal Congregationalism can deny the consciousness and practice of every right sentiment towards God and his Son. This theory, attempting to furnish in the best manner both Church and Congregation, in fact gives us neither. It narrows the former, loses hold of the latter, divides Christ himself, and secures but an imperfect Congregationalism after all. Of all ecclesiastical schemes beside, none, by not intentional, yet constitutional equivocation, so confounds realities and confuses the mind. Thus, by its doubling it is in contradiction with Christianity, science, nature, humanity, and simple theism itself. A Congregationalism that would justify its name can have but one whole body, belonging to the Lord by the very token of its common association and worship. The simplest inquisition would seem to settle this. What rational

Congregationalism will dare to consign to God's displeasure and to future woe any persons simply because they have not accepted the elements? Why, a man like Kane — who has made himself emphatically the person of our day, whom we know not whether to call hero or saint, Christian indeed as he was, yet such technically by right of birth and baptism alone — would on this principle be among the lost, instead of making north pole and tropic town alike two of the long steps by which all his earth-wandering became the straightest and most direct road to highest heaven.

Moreover, will a rational Congregationalism quite venture to stand sponsor for all to whom the elements have been allowed? Even if any denominations make this the sign of regeneration, and of passing from death unto life, will they in every case stand vouchers for the fact? If not, then is there not among us the corporate sin of a double mind? This query in the following treatise I shall present in particular relation to our views of the Supper. It is however proper I should say beforehand, that my method of argument will not be ecclesiastical, such in some sort although my subject be. Deliberately, at the hazard of disappointing those who may be inclined to examine my treatise with hope, and incurring an apparently triumphant censure from those who might in any case resist its doctrine, I choose for the most part less the historic than the ideal track. My course of investigation will not lead me mainly into that region of facts and texts, on whose low level and letter that killeth so many great themes lie swamped. Avoid ing the vicious circle of reasoning about a usage i the light of usage, let us go for our decisions, not t the fathers, but, if I may say so, to the Father. Hab it, our angel when good, is our demon when it is bad It is sad to have, like so many, no better reason fo doing a thing, than that we have done it a hundre times. I shall not therefore offer the case at the ba of that technical logic which is the retained advo cate and hired servant of every traditionary error Nothing has taken so many bribes and fees as ou logic. We are after all in our secret hearts gov erned less by our syllogisms than by our thoughts and I should not expect any one prepossessed with contrary persuasions to be convinced by whatsoeve ingenuity I might institute of debate. Let me rather if I can, raise the customs, of which I shall have to speak, into that higher light of ideas, which shows truth, as the higher law does duty, to our mind Imagination has a bad name among us. But I do not know that it errs more or oftener than what we call our reason. A true imagination is reason itsel in its highest function and form.

I am aware such a treatment may unfold my plan into a broad scope. If the particular topic seem in my handling to be often only a wedge to open larger and more radical inquiries into Christian truth and character, and the whole condition and wel fare of humanity, I trust, as the Church is in such strong possession and legal or influential pre-occupation of the world, this may prove not the least potent way in which such fundamental matters may be moved. If my method even lead me, as all that have a matter much at heart are well-nigh inevitably led, in maintaining my ground, seemingly to denounce others, let me say that I intend to bring only practices into question, and, so far as persons are concerned, charge no error of which I may not have been guilty myself.

I would trust, however, that there may be actually a humane as well as philosophic reason for this mode of treatment. I do not wish to write a book of controversy, least of all on matters tender to the Christian heart; but a volume in which any disciples might find something to read in connection with or preparation for the most affectionate exercises of their faith. I would even hope, beyond the rank of technical theologians, to interest some thinkers amid the great world, at which theology sometimes looks askance as evil, but which is the world of God's children and immortal souls. I would fain even take so wide a range as to adopt and baptize nature into the service and illustration of divine grace, believing these two radically exist, not in the contrast so often supposed, but in harmony, striking "with difference discrete" the same chord in the human heart, and calling back to each other in confirmation of God's truth, as deep answereth to deep through all his creation.

As the discussion proceeds, it will appear how a mere question of ecclesiastical procedure vitally involves our entire belief and conduct, our relation to God and man, — in fine, the complete proportion of the religious character, in a closing word upon which

I have not thought myself going too wide of the mark in view, according to a fair calculation of the best various points of aim. Through the round of topics may appear some repetition of thought. I am not anxious to make for it any apology. Not in number and multitude, but greatness and pertinence of thoughts, returning in diverse figures and combinations, is a book valuable; as the sweetness of a tune is made by its recurring theme, and changes in the same old days make the charm of Nature's volume and the unwearying melody of her speech.

With a pang of his own one presents what may pain others. But in stirring the thoughts of Christians to something better, there can be no evil-doing. The strain which any heaving at the anchor of our faith brings upon the whole man, the self-examination to which it fetches every one anew, the agitation or quarrel with the agitator, is not harmful, but for good. The angel that troubled Bethesda gave it its power to heal. I know that he who has left a ruin at the corner of my street is not a destroyer, but a builder. The design, the object, is all. An assassin throwing fulminating grenades, and a servant bringing candles, both deal in the same potent element of fire; and I understand myself to be striking a blow, not at, but for, the ordinance of communion, inasmuch as I believe it to be a time of peril for that ordinance, and that its salvation can be found in no exclusive system respecting it, but by making it the common property of all believers. It is weakened, and not established, by being esteemed a badge to identify the friends of Christ. But no hostility appears, save in a silent neglect; and a pastor, with a flourishing and harmonious people, has powerful reasons not to hazard active division and disturbance by raising any question on which there will certainly be two sides. What worldly motive can he have for disquieting himself? What folly not to keep rules as they came to him, and let his own growing prosperity alone! Ah! how often in this world has come fatal and blessed scattering of such calculations! The pastor is the leader of his flock. But his objection to close communion may first and most of all be, not as an administrator of the rite, but as a communicant. Why should he want to be doing what his very electors are not doing, — as though his doing it made or signified him to be more religious than they? He may feel too unworthy and too altogether like them to be able to bear the imputation. If so, let him eat what they eat, and drink what they drink, and be in fellowship with them, or else part peaceably.

Let us not forget how the ordinance has suffered by its own restrictions already. A considerable and undeniably Christian sect has in modern times omitted its use. A quarter-century ago a Unitarian clergyman, whose thought we may question but cannot despise, and whose name no tongue can truly take save with honor, left his profession because he could not administer it. In not a few really devout breasts still is disaffection to the rite, which any confinement of its privilege will only deepen and spread more wide, till — as no such authority can be pleaded for it as for the moral principles of the Gospel, as its defence must be in its practical benefits, and as every invidious limitation must go to neutralize them — at length the best piety of Christendom would leave it out of all reckoning to decline and die.

As I say this, let there be no indistinctness in my affirmation that, in any age yet at hand, I anticipate for it no such fate. A form is not, indeed, any more than is a rule of moral conduct, the highest thing in religion. But the Antinomianism which rejects all law is no ascent above morality. As history proves, it is rather the way to every abyss of dreadful license and excess. So anti-formalism for most men might lead to something quite different from spirituality. Accordingly there is as little of philosophy, and as little of humanity, as there is of Christianity, in throwing the form in question away.

Yet the freedom of abstinence from it, as of participation, should nowise be infringed. To attempt any compulsion either way over individuals or a society, is for ministers to try to be "lords over God's heritage." It is the right of every body of worshippers in the last resort to determine its own order of service. Surely, only after consultation with the people themselves, and with their sanction and encouragement, should any one in the ministry alter the established style. But, if the alteration can be made without violence, the inquisition of motives and ascertaining on what ground he stands, which it occasions in every man's bosom, will be but a new spring of life and common benefit. In the offer of open communion, the point of difficulty and debate is in declining to give the form of words by which they who officiate have been accustomed at once to invoke God's favor and separate two services from each other. The refusal, on any minister's part, to terminate the common exercises, when the worship is actually unfinished, by a phrase to the general understanding bearing the sense of dismission and actually bisecting the body, is no witholding of any benediction man can give, far less of the better blessing of God. To bless in such a case is to keep, not send away. In any society, it may notwithstanding be said, are those that cannot conscientiously receive the elements, and what but priestcraft and bigotry is it to attempt any arbitrary constraint! Can they not however conscientiously sit while others receive them? For the last year conversant with no small amount of discussion in every aspect of this theme, I have heard none say so; and if I did, I might ask how they can, as they are wont, conscientiously enter the meeting-house at all when the table is spread, and suffer the silver vessels to shine with the least lustre of symbolic meaning through their eyes. As it is all symbol, I confess my inability to comprehend the discrimination.

There may indeed be a natural and instinctive repugnance to change one's habits, which all persons feel, especially with growing years. There is doubtless an honest diffidence to take a position which can be understood as implying a growth of religious feeling one may be conscious of, yet unwilling to own. But the idea of violating his conscience because he witnesses a serious partaking of such an ordinance, which he himself has done his part to call the minister to uphold, can hardly lodge in a Christian's mind; and when the Communion shall vindicate its name as something common to the Lord's whole assembly, there can be certainly in regard to it no such shame, true or false. I trust there is even now more strength and health in all our consciences, than to refine the matter so much away from the honest procedure of our affections in all other things, as to discover in these emblems either a super-exalted sacredness we cannot touch, on the one hand, or a superstition and offence on the other.

In reserving, however, the rite to our list of the elect, the charge of unwarranted partiality we do incur. I know it is said thus only can we practically do. I have been repeatedly told, Your judgment of the case is perfectly true in principle; but it will not work well. You will get no more communicants than before. Indeed, one friend humorously continued, It almost seems as if we must have a little pretence, and even falsehood, in the Church, to get along most successfully with men, constituted as they are. To such suggestions I can only reply, that, although I believe open communion to be expedient, it is not on the ground of expediency, but of inevitable principle, that I have held it forth. It may be expedient to alloy gold for the currency of our traffic, and to have compromises in our political constitutions to make them march; and Lord Bacon, earthly-minded philosopher and guilty conformist to the world as he was, may say, if he will, that mankind is more pleased to look at truth in the deceptive shadows of gaudy lamps, than in the light of the sun. But, under our Master, we can know and speak only the truth, whether it slay or keep us alive.

I am sensible, moreover, it will be said, that all are not fit for this ordinance; that our Christian assemblies are not thoroughly Christian, save in name; that the world, in no good sense, is largely in the Church; in short, that my plan is to cast pearls before swine, forgetful of the depravity of mankind. I reply, depravity in our congregations is wholly out of place, an intruder and alien, in a circle where it does not belong, more than a conspirator belongs in the city, or an enemy's spy in the camp. It is not so much depravity as it is apostasy, just as hostility to our government by an American citizen is not simple war, but treason. The immigrant must be naturalized; but nurture, not naturalization, should make us members both of church and state. If indeed in any case there be no nurture, then, in the name of God and Christ, let conversion come!

Yet, in our congregations as they are, it is possible to animate and be all together warmed by the ordinance of the Supper, in its own original simplicity as a token, not a test. Opening it may not succeed immediately so well, as when a public sentiment, in the whole air of the Christian community, shall in this apparent exposure foster it, as sooner or later it assuredly will. Habit indeed is the most formidable castle. He that assails or would displace any custom, must look well to his armor. In this country especially, where all stand on a level, and every man in the mighty crowd is liable to be pushed by the weight of the entire mass, it requires more hardihood to stand up against a popular impression of any sort, than it does elsewhere in the world. So it is said there is perhaps more individual independence, though less liberty, in England than in the United States. It is not pleasant to quiet lovers of the shade, even for however little while, to be within the range of artillery. Few but would rather be posted where they might suffer no risk of being raked by those ecclesiastical guns, still handled, as once they were the most dreaded of all. But soldiers do not choose their own positions. Yet the figure is hardly just to those engaged in a movement which is not for war, but peace. It is for peace, because it is for union. Our old organization, however suited to a transition period, has grown corrupt, settling on the lees. Our ecclesiastical highways are full of ruts, and our travellers over them stuck fast in routine. All the people, as in the country, should turn out to mend the road to heaven.

Especially should we further the Christianizing of the world by the training of the generations of the young. A solemn dedication of themselves to God may well be made by adults that have grown up without spiritual culture. But let our children be given, and taught that they belong, to the Lord from the first. Regeneration is what we preach for the great doctrine. It is an experimental doctrine in more respects than one, demonstrated by the whole analogy of human relations. As their blind instinctive affection turns to an intelligent voluntary love, children are born again to their earthly parents; and what parental heart has not thrilled at the change? But who wishes it to be by a leap, instead of a growth? So let them be born again to God. Let the second birth, as is meet, be as orderly as the first. Born of the Spirit or wind, says Jesus, we must be. How then, in the type this language implies, is nature born again into blossom and flower in the air of heaven, at spring-tide? By a sudden spasm do the leaves come out, or are they mechanically picked open by our fingers? No, but in what living beauty of correct degrees! So be it with our spiritual unfolding. Then churches will not, like houses and ships, be built on worldly grounds, but consecrated indeed.

On this idea let us insist. Precious indeed is harmony. But let us have peace by the way of righteousness and truth, and value all things not formally, — rather according to their sincere worth. If we see, as we may, a church-steeple, which some malecontent rears over a place holding no worship, shall we reverence the steeple? If a legacy is offered inconsistent with the life of an institution, shall not the institution show its character and true dignity in declining with the terms the money its acceptance might make a bribe? If a famous dancer, with the nimbleness of her feet, carries up some of the stones of our Bunker-Hill Monument, shall we prize them as much as we do those which a pure patriotism contributes? At least no offering, which is not of the heart, affords strength to our worship.

We must, therefore, demand sincerity in our religious institutions, and of all concerned in them, at the outset. But, it is asked, are you not missionaries in the world? A Christian society is indeed a missionary body. But missionary within its own walls it can hardly be. Apologists plead that we must act from mixed motives; but will double-dealing at the start be likely to turn into frankness as we go on? Will truth, omitted without regret at the beginning of any enterprise, come into fashion and vogue on the way? Rather, owning endless degrees of sanctification and improvement, even unto a perfection that is divine, let us require the candor and devotion of discipleship under its name.

There are reasoners whose generalizations have carried them so far as to leave all names of Church or Christianity behind in contempt. But when the generalizing process can seduce a writer to the extent of declaring that there is no moral difference, worth considering, between one man and another, and leads a second writer to smooth over, as like a trifling roughness in the grain of the wood, the distinction between evil and good, a question may perhaps arise, alike in a religious or a philosophical mind, whether there is not some point for generalization to stop. If excessive particularizing makes the bigot with his narrow mind, or the superstitious man with his false reverence, too much generalizing empties the heart clean of its warmth, friendship, and worship. It abolishes all terms. It dissolves individual existences. It leaves the soul a mere subject, with no relations recognized to human creatures or to God himself.

One thinker may say, — I care for no ecclesiastical associations whatsoever, and find my only church in the world. But the world proves, as Jesus and his Apostles describe it, too wide, imperfect, and still evil, either to brace his holy efforts or give his spirit a home. He must, in contradiction of his theory, abide in and act from a grander, though in visible dimensions smaller circle, before he can act to bless and save the world itself.

Another thinker proclaims his allegiance to God in his pure infinity alone, leaving the Christ of the Gospel aside. But let his doctrine, of space and science and omnipresence of one solitary Power through earth and stars, recommend itself as it may to the speculative mind, it spreads a thin atmosphere around us, in which we feel discouraged and cold, like explorers of the Arctic region of thought, and cry out for a nearer and somehow more human divinity. This is the unspeakable boon Jesus confers on the human race, that he familiarizes and domesticates God, shows him in a mortal frame and in earthly homes, and by his incarnation of the Great Spirit makes us partakers of the Divine nature more than we could become by the discovery of ten thousand new systems, or peering for ever into the measureless expanse of the Milky-Way.

To individualize is as important as to generalize.

Is not the heart as great doing the first, as the head can be doing the last? He that ascends a mountain generalizes his view. But he loses sight of the house and the face of his friend. Let him stay an hour on the summit, but return to spend his days among the homes and persons it has pleased God, who cares for particulars, as well as generalities, to make! If we look at the infinite unity alone, like little creatures before leviathan, we are lost and devoured. But, in the element of freedom heaven pours out, we swim away. Difference and variety, whence comes the harmony of creation, have from the Maker a fine eternity too. It is easy to generalize. It is easy to collect facts. But to hold even in one's mind that balance of the universe wherein events and ideas, facts and laws, match and prove each other, and enlargement with illustration of truth goes for ever hand in hand, is very hard.

Let us avoid alike the pantheism that dissolves, and the idolatry that corrupts, worship and all virtue. Let us walk on that Mahomet's bridge, — sharp and thin as a razor, into paradise, — which is made of the use of means, yet not putting the means for the end. On the wings of all the winds come news of a great revival of religion in the land. Heaven grant the soul fail not of the promised good, by resting in that verbal, ritual, social display of the religious sentiment, of which Jesus is so jealous; but that the last, most delicious and satisfying fruit of a new spirit of humanity be increased on the topmost and outermost branches of the tree of life, in addition to all the lesser virtues that hang on its lower boughs! If piety be the foundation, charity is the top-stone of the Christian character; and the lifting of the one, as in our stone towers, is as important and as worthy to be celebrated as the other. If prayer be the first, humanity is the last virtue. Men learn to be obsequious to God long before they learn to be just to one another. The whole East, in the gray morning of the world, blazes with the universal watch-fire of adoration. The biggest books of the Persians, Indians, Hindoos, are of what but worship! Slowly and late, as the race travels from the garden it was born in to the setting sun, opens the humane sentiment. Almost everywhere, among Chinese, Japanese, French, English, Americans, Turks, Christians, we see contempt, the disposition to despise each other, the fear to mix with one another, lest their several principles should be lost and manners corrupted. How soon children learn to look down on children! How age with failing memory drops years of momentous history, but no fact of vanity! We make our self-consciousness the boundary of the universe. He that scorns none is great and good. When shall the day come for men and women to show the grand courtesy to human nature, as well as homage to the Divine, which was the characteristic of Jesus Christ alone in the world? Among the reasons stated for the formation of one of our most venerable churches was, that men might lay aside that relation of experiences elsewhere imposed for admission to the Lord's table. It was alike a respect to the Holy Spirit and a tribute to the human soul. Could I do anything to encourage a humane life and temper, as well as devotional forms, for the Christian's last and surest mark, — could I show the Master's walk as the direction in which to look for God, and the Master's form as not coming between us and the Father to hinder or obscure, but transparent with deity, — not in vain, to those accustomed to hear or willing to read what I say, should I dedicate these words.

CHURCH AND CONGREGATION.

CHAPTER I.

DESIGN.

The present work has originated in no presumption of its author to reform the Church, and in no trouble of his own parish, but in a personal difficulty within himself. He imagines for his word no such influence in the community as would justify his volunteering questions of essence so vital and reach so wide as he has been led to discuss. Any man's benevolence must consider the sphere it can fill, and the ends it can attain, before it starts on its way; else it may soon prove something quite different from real benevolence, of a spirit however warm and honest it may be.

Therefore I must retreat to a deeper ground, and however, like others, trusting that love for fellow-creatures is an ever-present and all-comprehending motive of procedure, yet assume in this particular matter no good-will of which private conscience has not sharply touched the springs. Still, as a man's meeting even a cross in his way would not excuse his telling of it, but only hanging upon it if truth required, I should say nothing in public of what has perplexed myself, did I not know of many others, clergy and laity, likewise perplexed. How unambiguous and daily more extensive the signs that the constitution of the Congregational Church, as a twofold body divided by a formal line, — or that part only regarded as Church which the line includes, and all outside as but the world, — is falsely representing the Christian facts, inflicting pain on true piety, offending the religious judgment of the best persons, in the diminution of communicants throughout New England, showing a loss of its hold on the conscious respect of the human mind, and, in fine, shall I not say grieving the Holy Spirit of God! The Roman

Church, the Greek Church, the English Church, though all but sects of Christianity, at least aim at the unity the Apostolic Church had. The Puritan Church in our own land, signing off from all Episcopal motherhood, owned itself but one body, acting in a civil and ecclesiastical capacity, church and town at once, identified every way with the kingdom of God.

But Dissent, as a whole, while asserting the freedom of thought, bearing the line of judgment more than the bond of affection in its hand, and using the English Independency, the Scotch Presbytery, and the Genevan and New England Calvinism for its instruments, has with all its advantages joined this evil of cutting asunder the company of followers Jesus never so divided, with a ritual knife. What is the spectacle which the Congregational minister, at every celebration of the Lord's Supper, periodically beholds? He is deserted on the spot by a vast majority of those by whom, very commonly, in our days, as proprietors of the church, he has actually been elected to his post, and appointed to do every office, even that single one left to this scantling of the assembly behind! His monthly joy becomes his monthly sorrow, in the troops that file out and the thin ranks that stay. Wherefore, he asks, so is or must it be? Are the remaining ones the only Christians, lovers of God and followers of his Son? No; he recognizes in the departure qualities that had illumined the house of God with a lustre quite as bright as the spirituality which waits can cast on the table of the Lord. He finds the ordinance no Aaron's censer that he may shake between the living and the dead. As a badge of sanctity and a separation from iniquity, he sees proof overwhelming within and without the charmed circle, that it fails.

If the rite does not decide as between individuals the question of general excellence, does it not at least mark out with its plummet those who have the particular graces of faith and love to Christ? No; he sees friends of Christ, if Christ has any friends, from the ceremonial going away. Beyond all show or sound of forms, their life and conversation, countenance and manner, look and tone, are the best pictures to portray and the most moving eloquence to bespeak this truth. The minister liberalizes his invitation, perhaps imposes no covenant, exacts no promise, makes no examination, and propounds no name. But his charity is scarce heeded, save by some solitary strangers, pleased with a greeting, it may be unwonted and in an unaccustomed place, while multitudes of the best friends and supporters of the whole institution of worship still perseveringly afflict him as they retire. Why should they not? Immediately upon his words of welcome, the minister stretches his arms for the assembly to rise, and pronounces the phrase called a Benediction, but which, with the force of tradition, for ages widely through Christendom has in the popular mind borne the sense of a dismission. So true is this, that the language is often as naturally styled a dismission as a blessing. It says to the general company, save such of them as have observed some special ecclesiastical condition, *come* and *go*, in the same breath! It is like the Finis of a volume. The tardy church-goer, — who, meeting the crowd dispersing at the door and inquiring if all was done, was told, All is *said*, but remains to be done, — had at least conveyed to him in the witticism, that the benediction was understood to terminate the free and open service of the building. But what a strange and self-contradictory function of a blessing, to rive a worshipping body asunder! For one, with no such purpose can I utter it. A true blessing must operate to bind, not sever, all who receive it. Certainly *the grace of the Lord Jesus Christ, and the love of God, and the communion and fellowship of the Holy Spirit,* — whose ancient and hallowed phraseology has been so self-contradictorily used to scatter so many religious assemblies, at the division of which all over the world an affectionate Christian imagination can but shudder, — should be employed rather for such a healing and catholic end, that its precious burden may henceforth roll only in music and peace and bliss on the ears of mankind.

I know it may be said, in respect to many of our churches, only those leave who choose, and all may stay who please. It is my extreme doubt whether, with the ordinarily understood meaning of a benediction, this can be justly alleged. If so, why do they depart? The scrutiny of motives is always a delicate, and should be a very modest and respectful task. Some may hold themselves unfit for an exercise superstitiously esteemed more sacred than any devotion, confession, or hallelujah beside. Some may be looking forward to it when their resolves shall be strengthened and their thoughts cleared. Some young persons, touched with the beauty of the Lord, may but be waiting till they can be regarded as old enough to partake. Some may feel an inconsistency between the tenderly solemn scene and their surrender to the business and pleasures of the world, though, in this case, their assumption of harmony between these latter and the sublime owning of the Almighty in his temple would have still to be explained. Inquisitive and sceptical persons may ask if the entire ritual be not a Jewish antiquity, preposterously out of place and date among us and in the circumstances of modern life,—something fit in the old East, but not agreeable to the Occidental mind.

But through all these diverse views runs that visible distinction into more and less Christian, loving, and holy, on the basis of which many can never persuade themselves to separate from the congregation and be united to the church. For one, clergyman as I am, I thank God that, upon this construction of the case, they cannot! For this formal division into the more and less holy in the name of Christ, is an unchristian thing. Nor could I consent, by an outward technical act, to say I love Christ better than do others, any more than I could denominate myself in general holier than they: for what moral or spiritual quality is greater, or of a loftier claim, than a true love of Christ? An external certificate of love and purity — as goods are stamped and warranted, often how deceptively, in the market, or as men know their living property in those other flocks that symbolize the Christian ones in the pasture and field — is least welcome to natures the most delicate and refined. As from an abomination, they shrink from whatever has the least color of courtiership and favoritism with the Most High.

The only escape from these embarrassments seems to be taking up the line by which the company is torn apart; abolishing all notion either of mystery or exclusiveness in the special service; opening it, as not possibly more holy than the all-embracing, none-excluding adoration of the Infinite One, to the congregation's eye and ear and heart; leaving the participation of the elements free to every one's discretion in the sight of God; while the servant at the altar, if he does so regard the Lord as offering his supper to every soul, declines by word or act of his to be an organic part of the falsehood, which every restriction within the common body of believers implies. Doubtless this course is rightfully to be taken with the consent and concert of those in the affair equally concerned with the minister, who is but one of the brethren discharging a particular function in the church; for upon any attempt to constrain, contrary to his conscience, his procedure, he has, in this country, the resource of resigning his place always open; and it is better for him, as for everybody, to starve than to lie.

For the stand thus indicated I propose to give in the following treatise my reasons more at large. It will appear, I trust, that what I intend is not innovation, but primitive and for ever true Christianity; not a fresh heresy broached, but an inveterate one shut up and destroyed. Far enough am I from being in my position alone. Were it consistent with the simplicity of my work to publish testimonials offered me, these pages would not only have an authority, nothing of which my name can add, but a power of composition beyond the compass of my pen. As the writer of these lines well remembers, that brother of a noble religious genius, Sylvester Judd, whose body has for five years lain in his lamented grave, when his last illness seized him, had on his very mouth a word to utter among us in confirmation of what he had already so ably said and done for the unity of the Church. Who can doubt such, too, would have been the issue of Channing's thought? But I will not enumerate names, arguments though they be; but only pray God from what I have written to winnow the chaff, if there be any wheat.

CHAPTER II.

POSITION.

THAT the Christian Body is rightfully not twofold, but one, as a generality none may dispute, though of the sense of this unity there will be as many interpretations as there are denominations to arrogate each the true Church as identical with itself. While, therefore, the double *practice* of sects and nominal Christians, who violate the unity in which they believe, is open to rebuke as a common sin of mankind, for the double *theory* of Congregationalism I know not what defence can be set up. We have church and congregation. But which is the true original body? The Greek term, *ecclesia*, is more properly rendered congregation or assembly of persons called together; and the learned and noble-minded Bunsen declares the Church to be nothing but the Christian congregation. Yet, whatever style of company was first, and whatever term be truest, it is clear there was only one body, and no duplicity or doubleness of constitution, among the first disciples of Jesus.

Beside, although as early as the third century the division may have begun, a feeling of the error of all schism seems to have haunted the consciousness of the Church in every age. Heresy itself, in the Scripture construction, is, not free thought or private judgment, but a rending of the living body of the Lord; and so it is the grandest praise of the Romish communion, that, with all its corruptions and tyrannies, it has so largely succeeded in vindicating to itself as characteristic the title *Catholic*, after Christian the highest epithet, best naming the bond between the human and divine. Not for this alone, surely, would I join the Romish fellowship, or abjure my glorying in a Protestant descent; but only with a filial sorrow criticise Protestantism,— the mother of freedom, science, good government, civilization, and social prosperity,— that she has admitted disunity so widely into her very scheme, and allowed charity so greatly to fall out of her lap.

In maintaining that Christ's body should not be formally divided, I do not, however, make any disparagement of ecclesiastical ceremonies, far less of the principle of form in the Church. To her, as to every existence in the universe, form is necessary, and, for her beauty and thriving, exercises must be distinct and various. But how eagerly the old Churchy earned to include and set at one all her members, and adopt for her children the universal offspring of God, is seen in the fact of its having in her precincts been almost as much a matter of course to be baptized as to be born; and our forefathers, treading her idolatries under their feet, yet retained in their order this rule of unity, till, in the tide of free-thinking scepticism and revolutionary pass on, that whelmed civil and religious things together, it was swept away. That no outward circumstance constitutes, though it may issue from church-membership, our whole reasoning, as I trust, will clearly evince; but on grounds of the evident intention, shape, and drift of ecclesiastic usage as a whole, as well as the firmer primeval basis of Christian principle, might be framed a conclusive argument against that twofold division of the Church which only the fraction of a few that come out, to use the vulgar phrase, would seriously wish to produce and perpetuate. The soul of tradition, in what the Church has striven to hand down, is for unity, whatever any particular tradition may be. Ecclesiastical history tells us that even children partook of the Lord's Supper till the twelfth century; certainly it is time no longer from the very sight of the supper to send them away!

One who sees, or in authentic annals reads, how particular local customs have sprung up, may well marvel at the superstitious exaggerations which would hold the Lord's influence dependent on some accurately preserved custom or polity, whose direct tendency may be to make his commandment of none effect, yet whose disuse is trembled at as nothing less than breaking his sceptre, and interrupting his reign on the earth. Truly he has better watch of his influence than this! Not so subservient is the Lord! Ecclesiastical schools have easily and inveterately quarrelled about the precise genuine shape of the Church, because its Founder gave it no exact earthly shape. There is no authorized, everlasting mode of religious action. There is no tribunal to settle the dispute. Hopeless indeed in its continuance must it be! The Author and Finisher of our faith took care that his principles should be clear in their infinite scope, but left the organization to be created, altered, and enlarged in their unfolding. Only that administration would displease him which divides the flock, and would part sworn brothers and very friends; and for this sin modern brotherhoods in name, as well as ancient bishoprics and popedoms, have answer before man and God to make, — for from the bar of brethren sentences of as cruel wrong have been meted out, as in the conclave of cardinals or the star-chamber of a king. The fan that religious reformers have borne in their hand has been wielded so fiercely, as sometimes to blow solid and sweet sanctity no less than worthless refuse away, as a high wind scatters the kernels the husbandman only proposed to separate from the straw. Such a fan has been and is at work in drawing between one and another portion of believers the Lord's Supper as a line. Let the Church be one, and the fan relinquished from human hands and restored to Him who alone can and "will thoroughly purge his floor." Liberty is not a necessary sacrifice to union in the Church, nor union to liberty, but both these will be one and the same when despotism and license, twin-born, alike disappear.

Meantime, can a small and aged minority of the worshippers in any place, or a collection or series of such minorities dispersed over the earth's meridians and parallels, be considered the whole Church of Christ? This the fruit of eighteen hundred years? No, — in the name of Him who built it on a rock, affirmed in it a perpetuity and power against which the gates of hell should not prevail, knew beside it no other association in the terms of his Gospel, and, by nobler words than the knighthood of chivalry was ever conferred from royal bounty, made little ones the conquerors of the earth to his reign! Church and congregation indeed cannot be severed, members of the former being of course members of the latter, though a particular external abstinence alone may cause that members of the latter shall not be members of the former. But these compartments are not features of Christ's building, only wings added thereto. We speak of Scripture interpolations. This distinction is a Church interpolation.

Moreover, it contradicts the consciousness of the Church itself, purer and nearer Christ's mind by far now, than in the third and fourth centuries. A discontent with it of the intelligence of the day, and even of the general mind, is, spite of the growth of population, actually sapping the foundations of the Church; and should the process which has begun go on, the Church, in our accredited understanding of it, will by the flow and pressure of public opinion be disintegrated in a period as calculable as the wearing away of the porous rock under the roll of Niagara. Yet the real Church is not to be wasted, but rescued for ever alive.

As many minds at once hover on the verge

of all discovery, descrying new planets, detecting new substances for use and new arts for human advancement or relief; so out of the confused ideas and inconsistent conditions of our epoch, in which, as at an earlier era, every one has his own psalm or interpretation, book or order of service, — among which varieties every collection of believers has its own style of the Supper, different invitations or terms preliminary to the feast prevailing in not a few different assemblies even of the same denomination, — we may hope principles will emerge reconciling with law our liberty; and of these do I err in placing foremost, in the prophetic longing of this time, open communion? As the rigor of theological creeds is relaxed, as the sacredness from ecclesiastical formulæ departs, as religion becomes less an opinion and more a life, as, like an ill-accommodated resident, it moves its too long inhabited quarters in the metaphysical brain, and takes lodgings in the heart, — all which it must do before the growing knowledge and charity of our day, — this consummation will gradually come. No unpardonable sin certainly against the Holy Ghost can that be considered which is at once the first doctrine and last aim of the Gospel, — the ample port which already, though dimly, shines from afar to receive the long-tost vessel of our faith.

Not in one sect alone, reckoned liberal or latitudinarian, do the signs point to open communion, instead of what, with singular incongruity between the substantive and adjective, we call *close*. It is noteworthy that in that great and most respectable Baptist connection of dissenters, specially addicted to the latter mode, the new London Whitefield, beyond any modern preacher beside drawing the multitudes with his voice, should have proclaimed against all opposition his conversion to the former, beginning to open the door, though he may not be prepared to open it wide. Our own history in the matter is *nothing* but prediction of the same result, fulfilling itself. It would be a curious and long account to trace the various scarcely interrupted steps of change ever to greater truth as well as generosity in this matter, in the single line of our own theological descent, from a practical union of church and state among our forefathers, through half-way covenants, formal candidates, solemn vows, subscriptions of arbitrary creeds, or examinations before formal councils and appointed defenders of the faith, to the simple private conversations with a friendly pastor, by which the doorway to the Lord's table has been successively and ever more slightly guarded against rash or unfit intruders; while far back of us in historic thought, though near in space, lie the Romish theories of mystery, transubstantiation, and sacrifice, of whose half Jewish, half Pagan genius millions have taken so long ago their leave.

If now I venture an announcement of the time at hand to plant no sentinel at the Lord's table more than at the temple-gate, as he has sent out no word to plant any; if I maintain the Supper, like every other exercise in God's house, to be a means of spiritual benefit, free to all who worship the Father in the Saviour's name, I trust the event will show such declaration no broader than its abundant proof. A means I shall endeavor to prove it, and such I presume not a few of my readers consider it to be. If then it fall into the category of means instead of ends, to whom in Christendom shall it not be available? Even if its celebration be in a certain sense one of the ends for which the Church is constituted, yet, as the great philosopher Kant so finely says, an organized body has this for its very definition, that all its ends are means.

The Christian times in which we live, universalizing every sort of good in the very spirit of Him who asked the Pharisees if they could not read the indications of their own day, demand this church extension, not in new edifices only, but new sympathy within the edifices reared. I say this with no implication of self-righteous censure against customs of a former date. Let the dead bury their dead, and each age of humanity before God stand or fall in the light of his own conscience. When priest Ambrose shut in the face of Emperor Theodosius the holy portals whose decaying particles are said in their bronze successors to be yet preserved, as we clamp in iron the rotting limbs of liberty-trees emblematic of great events in our political annals, the act may have been but a protest against despotism, suited to the exigency of the case. Perhaps now there are things, if not persons, that should not be admitted to the temple, out of which Jesus drove the cattle and trading thieves. Nevertheless the general glory of the Church is its unlimited accessibility to the sons of men. Its true defence, unlike that of a fort or castle, is in its open gates. Its conquest is only winning. When Satan was let loose in the raging tempest of human passions, it may have been requisite to build its walls high and thick, as common dwellings of the Middle Ages still standing were made, like prisons, with grated windows, to guard against assassins' and soldiers' attacks.

But the Church has made its position in the world good. The ark of God has brought its treasure of humanity safe through the old flood of evil. It is time for men to leave its narrow chambers and accommodate themselves in more spacious homes alike consecrated to him. The health and power of the Church lie now in lifting every window and clearing every passage. It needs no outward seven-fold shield of Achilles to protect its peculiar life. *My pulpit has no doors*, said a great-hearted preacher, pointing his brethren of another name to its wide, unclosed entrances, which seemed, as he spoke, gateways both for the ocean and the land. It will be a happy day when no shrine or cathedral shall have within its space, more than at its front, enclosures of official sanctity or bars of a fancied material Holy of Holies. The design of the Church, different from that of a fortified place, is not repulse, but welcome. To redeem the world, not turn it into an ecclesiastical establishment, is Christ's aim. For this the Church is but an instrument in his hand. It is not itself God's kingdom, but the road thereto. God's kingdom is the whole world of human avocations and affections consecrated to him in the obedience of his laws; and the Church is not the object and business of mankind, any more than the compass is the ship, the rudder the cargo, or the chart the voyage.

The world was not made for the Church, but the Church for the world. Christianity itself is not all. It were partial and superstitious to say it is. Rather, as its Author and Finisher said, it is a leaven cast into the flood and mixture of human affairs, and depths of the human heart, for unbounded spread of sanctity and power. It is a high school of human nature, not a monopoly of the soul. It is a circular reaching through the earth, not a railed space upon it. Bible and Gospel, as Jesus said of the Sabbath, are made for man, not man for them.

Surely I would not so generalize our religion as to make it practically nothing while seeming to make it everything. It is not everything. It distinguishes things. Nothing is such a distinguisher. It runs that line between evil and good which men in their selfishness, low passion, and political corruption try to rub out, and would expunge from the record, but that by the Almighty finger it is so keenly drawn that they only wear themselves away who seek to obliterate it. To fall or be fallen upon by "this stone," is alike fatal. Christianity, peculiar, selecting some things, rejecting others, unable to give up or adulterate its own essence, cherishing only what it can appropriate, yet has an assimilation of unparalleled potency, like the digestion that can turn gravel and poison into vigor and food. Beyond the boasted national patriotic quality that can make of every race Americans, is its virtue to convert all tribes into Christians. It takes the mass of bewildered men in the midst of pollution to transform into its everlasting life. Like the seed, with its metamorphosis of dust into fragrant bloom, has its seminal living and life-giving property proved. Nothing in the world, that stains, has been able to stain it. Snow-white is the scarlet sin, and as wool the crimson iniquity, in its wondrous hand. Ignorance, barbarism, superstition, idolatry, touched by it, deny their nature, put on its dignity, shine with its light, are transmuted into its love. It is going to wash all mankind of their defilements, and refashion them after the pattern of their Lord.

But its great visible agency is the Church, friend, though antagonist, of the world. It is said of Jonathan Edwards, that, seeing the

Church relent towards the world, he rushed in and made the breach irreparable. But irreparable it is not. They must be brought together. The huge Goliath shall be overcome by the Son of David. The loose, fickle, unprincipled, vast world shall be won by the inseparable, immortal band of the righteous, sooner and more surely than they scattered or consumed by its flames or delusions. Little is the fine salt to the bulky earth it seasons. Of how small a lustre of his disciples Jesus declared it was the light of the world! The small minority of ten good men saves the city. So the Church shall triumph. Not, however, by any rigid shape or mode of action will this be. The fable of the heathen deity, Proteus, shifting into many a figure, and more formidable for every change, may teach the lesson of moral prowess which Paul, indeed the great missionary, truthfully practised, being, for the truth, all things to all men. If the Church be divine, as we believe, and the gates of hell shall not prevail against it, it may safely allow within reach of its communion and the mighty alterative of its grand and heavenly power all human souls.

CHAPTER III.

REASON.

I HAVE explained the scope of my plan. But no general speculations will suffice to settle any point of Christian doctrine or practice. For what reason, then, should congregation and church be identified, or, to particularize the question, why should the Lord's Supper be open to all Christian worshippers? I answer, because Jesus himself opened it to his disciples, irrespective of their vast diversities. From his special request that they would *all* drink of the cup, it would seem as if they might not all have eaten of the bread, certainly that he would have no one present with him omit the symbol. From him surely the Romish communion for the people *in one kind* has no authority. That he made it no test of creed, judgment on character, line between church and congregation, but a memorial of love alone, appears from the slightest examination. Who were they to whom he administered it? The twelve apostles, Luke says, were with him at the table. Among them, certainly not dismissed before he had received a savory morsel from Christ's own hand, was Judas the traitor, with Peter the denier, Thomas the unbeliever, and all the company to be cowardly deserters, yet all invited guests. By whatever recognition of their regard for Jesus we may qualify this judgment, we cannot escape the fact of their vast diversity of disposition, confidence in the Master's cause, and respective moral worth. Peter, the most ardent of the disciples, proved the most fearful, and John, the most gentle, approached nearest to being brave. It has been asked, If Jesus meant to open his supper to all, why did he not invite persons from Jerusalem and all Judæa to the feast? The question does not consider how few there were to call; that Christ's open adherents and regular attendants, through whom he would promulgate his religion, were all with him, and that the measure of Jewish hospitality toward him was scarce more ample than the precincts in which the feast was spread. But the width of its intent appears from the character of the festival to which it succeeded. As all Jews celebrated the Passover, he would have all Christians observe the Supper.

Confirmatory evidence arises from the opening of the Supper in the early Apostolic Church. Even for eating and drinking condemnation in excesses of intoxication and gluttony, by which the Corinthian rich separated themselves at the altar from the fasting poor, Paul forbids none to come to the table, but rebukes them in order to their reform. That afterwards the Supper was made a mystery, a thing for a few, as a natural relic or politic offset for Pagan mysteries, is surely no cause we should keep it such, unless we will find in any established corruption itself argument for its own continuance.

But furthermore, supposing it desirable to have a service distinguishing betwixt the faithful and the recreant, the Supper fails, and by the philosophy of human nature must fail, to answer this purpose. A man recognizes his property, as it floats in the river or moves in the pasture, by an outward stamp; but there is no earthly certificate of goodness, and the moment a man thinks he possesses it, he falls from the grace of Him whose spotless soul revolted at the thought of being called good. There is a difference, indeed, says a late German writer, between being good and being conscious that I am good! To be good is doubtless the greatest of all things in earth or heaven. To be conscious that we are good, is to fall like a Pharisee on earth or Lucifer from the sky. Christ indisputably was good; but refused to own the consciousness or accept the praise of being such, neither having his own nor adopting another's opinion of his character, precisely because the character was so pure. The saintly prayer, *Lord, if there be in me anything good, grant I may never know it*, may be extravagant; but it is not true or Christian to designate one's self as good in comparison with others. There is in fact no visible trace, like a diamond-point on glass, to break society in two, one side the friends of Jesus, the other his foes. There is a distinction among men, as the soul knows, — a distinction Christianity sharpens, not wipes out; but no formal line of distinction can be ecclesiastically drawn coincident with the real one. So, saith the Scripture, judge not!

But were it possible, it is not desirable so to divide. Those wonted to the feast would or ought to shrink from regarding it as their profession of holiness, or a brand of shame on its neglecters, thus committing those sins apostles'. pens score, and Christ thunders at, of sanctimony and censorious judgment. *God,* said one, *knows who the clergymen are!* God knows his children and his Son's disciples. God will set the sheep on his right hand and the goats on his left, so that no more than any other diverse kinds in his creation they can be confounded. For what reason are sheep or goat, viper and serpent, wolf and fox, lamb and dove, used as symbols in the Bible, but to indicate the fixed and determinate difference between moral good and evil by quoting animal species, the impossibility of whose being confounded is known alike to the wise man's science and the fool's or ignorant man's common sense? But who will antedate the decision, unseat the bar of judgment from its clear, lofty place, and plant it among earthly shadows and doubts? For individual protection and guidance, private estimates of our fellow-creatures are unquestionably requisite. Human law must pass on overt acts of crime for the safety of the common weal. But the Divine wisdom and mercy for human love and peace allow in no man's hand a plummet for the motives, or a measuring-band of the responsibilities and constitutional capacities, of human souls. Almighty justice reserves, against all appeal, such jurisdiction to the superior court. Blessed be the Judge, there is no absolute balance trusted to the hands of any corporation, — Pope, cardinals, bishops, synods, — but only what his finger suspends!

Beside, to separate, if we knew them, the evil from the good, would but contradict Him who rooted not the tares from the wheat, who ate with publicans, consorted with sinners, talked with the woman Pharisees would have stoned, suffered poor Mary Magdalene to commune with him indeed, and in her own act to paint a picture there in Judæa, to the envy of Greek and Italian masters, in never-fading colors, as she washed his feet with her tears and wiped them with the hairs of her head. The Lord's Supper for the perfect alone? He had no errand to them at all! His whole mission, and every means of grace he brought from heaven, were for earth-bound and unworthy souls. The cry of no union with sinners, be their sins personal, social, or political, is unchristian and inhuman: fully carried out, it would break up every civil community, rend asunder every neighborhood, dissolve every family, inflame every friendly circle, and, in that dualism of the soul old philosophers and New Testament writers describe, put every man at variance with himself.

God's design, furthermore, on the world's whole theatre, agrees with Christ's institution, in mingling human beings together for common good. As husband and wife are joined for better or worse, as their descendants, however unlike, hold fast one another, as the dying man, faint but eager, while before the pallor of his face the tide of life ebbs, and his limbs grow cold, and his tongue dumb, looks from his bed after all his children, though he may love some one more fondly, so our Head would unite us. There is no better title for a church than that sometimes chosen, of "All Souls," — which, God says, are his. The exclusive or partial administration of the Lord's Supper is a mutilation of the Church. The more splendid a work of art, the uglier the flaw that makes its beauty the worst of ruins. The nobler the mountain or cliff, the sadder the fissure by which it crumbles away. That the grandest association on earth, unlike Christ's robe that was woven without seam, and his body not a bone of which was broken, should exist under any sort of duplicity, is a misfortune and injury indeed!

Yet, again, why should not the Supper be open equally with any other religious rite? What reason can be stated for putting it on any different footing from that of the general worship and praise? No ordinance constitutes the Church. No participation in any ordinance constitutes membership in the Church. The ordinances are practices not constituents of the Church, things which its members, made such by the love and faith of Christ, use as symbols and exercises of such love and faith. In order to be united by faith and love, must persons expressly say or write it down that they are so united? Is the union which constitutes the Church dependent on, and caused by, any profession? No, that is to put the outside before the inside, and postpone the cause to the effect. It is not the circumstance, but the animating spirit, that consecrates any place or service. If one of our brothers in Christ finds his last rest in the desert, shall not Arabian sands be holy? Our loyalty to our Master is our personal following, not giving a sign like a military signal or password. Alas! when the stress is laid on that, how often in all religious or secular history it has by treachery been falsified to issues most dreadful of slavery, cruelty, and blood!

Is it said, into the widely opened door hypocrites may enter? But do they not into the narrowly closed one? With most likely success will they not present themselves at the most jealous entrance of the "most straitest sect," to get the highest repute of godliness they desire? There is no hole so small but the hypocrite will choose to push through, rather than go in with a crowd at the lofty gateway; and though stupid lower creatures may be restrained by fences of wood or wire, no hedge has yet been invented to keep him, the subtle and cunning man, out. Alas! this enemy of moral growth, like the artful insect foes of the beauty and fruitfulness of our gardens and fields, chiefly infests the denominations most ascetic and severe, and within their thorny bars mainly flourishes in show of all virtue and odor of sanctity. But if to this or any other religious rite, spite of any officers of the ecclesiastical custom stationed to detect and exclude with their most searching tests an adulterate or contraband spirituality, hypocrites after all do and will come, who shall identify or sentence them but He to whom we every one stand or fall?

If we apply a test of Christ's true Church, it must not be a ceremonial one; for though the Church has ceremonies, it is not a ceremonial body. Far more, it is a believing, loving, working body, composed of those toiling, spending, sacrificing for their fellow-creatures, mercifully giving, personally serving, visiting poor men and prisoners, clothing the naked as they ply the needle, — for humanity more blessed, though little instrument in woman's hand, than the cannon which at man's hostile touch has roared over this stage of time, — sending the Gospel to the heathen, or emigrant children to Western homes, or gathering for instruction the ignorant from our own streets. With them we are in the Church, though the room be no temple or cathedral, but plain as that beyond the Mediterranean Sea where Christ's followers were first assembled. Among the good I am in the Church more than amid the shine of sacred vessels or sound that reverberates from the ceiling or hangs its echoes in celestial arches. Ah! the Church, as a visible corporation, has not searched out or known all the members of Christ's body at every humble and holy task of brain and heart and feet and hands throughout the world. She may be a mother, saying of famous and canonized children with more than the old matronly joy, *These* are my jewels. But the jewels seen by the eye of God and cherished by the lowly king of Israel for his crown she has completely neither counted nor prized!

Once more, the Supper should be open to all Christian worshippers because it is a symbol; and it is the very nature and genius of a symbol to bring human beings together. Dogmas divide: emblems unite. Witness the family name, political motto, common seal, national flag, humane watchword! A hundred barbarian tribes from thousand-fold conflict and division flock to one Roman banner, and march under its single magnificent blaze. Secret societies by their signals last for ages. A domestic memorial or escutcheon draws tears when the bosoms that bravely bore it beat no more than other dust. A picture, ornament, anniversary, binds children in one over the ashes of dead parents, — shall I not say, rather, under the eyes of living ascended ones? It draws, by some mysterious suggestion, human bond, electric chord, upon those associations of kindred blood in a common nature, to which few persons are insensible, or for insensibility to which we count no man better, however sage, and in whatsoever respect above his fellows he may be. But no signal like the Lord's Supper has marshalled the zeal and courage of the world, as to the religion's first imperial leader the sky-flaming cross announced, *In this sign thou shalt conquer!* How many tribes and tongues have followed after it! Said the famous Hungarian, whose speech, more than that of any other modern orator, lately shook the world, *If our foes drive us to it, we will eat the Last Supper and go down to the field of death!*

In fine, does not the spectacle of the prepared ordinance itself invite all? At what invisible line of peril on the floor should any one start, as, by some old remembrance of fright or stumbling, a human being or lower creature is startled or shies at a particular undiscernible point in the road? The very notion of that invisible line, as a line we or any one but God can run, let us take away!

As between individuals in this world, it was never meant for us by any concert of pretended religion to draw. Jesus himself drew lines only between diverse classes, not stigmatizing particular persons to consign them to their doom. Many are the evils, and great the wrong, of our doing otherwise. The idea especially of different sets of obligations for different classes of Christians, according as they do or do not frequent the Lord's table, let us abjure, as not only superstition, but demoralization. The custom of dismissing all children as unfit to witness the scene, significant of the inextinguishable love of their Saviour and best friend, let us straightway honor in the breach thereof: for who more than they should be addressed by the natural, beautiful, silent language of commemoration, till they are gradually trained at parental discretion to participate all the more intelligently and beneficially in what so long their feelings shall have apprehended and their senses observed.

Let us, in this matter, act after the truth and nature that dictate all our other common proceedings. If you had some touching celebration in your own dwelling, would you send the children away, or have even the babe brought in arms and the very infant in its cradle dragged in to be present? Why then leave the growing generation out of this divine pathetic teaching? Why in it should husbands forsake their wives, brothers their sisters, offspring their parents? It will be very difficult for members of Christian societies or Christian principles to answer that question, why. But that it may at least be heard and considered, is the purpose for which I write. Its true answer I believe to be a practical one, and only this: — Let us be all together in that Jesus meant for nothing but to bring us together. Never till we are so brought, shall we be truly what he designed in his Church.

CHAPTER IV.

SYMBOL.

A SYMBOL, as I have said, is a thing by its very nature uniting all who believe what is symbolized. It is all the more one of the curious solecisms of human experience, that symbol, in our religion, suited as it is to engage the imagination, appealing to the heart, and being a common language everywhere independent of the Babel of spoken tongues, should have been used, not to universalize, but limit Christianity. As not a few take the ground that the ordinance of the Supper, so far from being designed for a general privilege of his followers, was simply a temporary and provisional matter in Christ's own plan, never intended for continuance, and that its perpetuity in time, far more its extension through the Church, is a purely arbitrary superstition, let me proceed to maintain that the symbolic nature of the rite, as it belongs to all who accept its significance, certifies its enduring purpose and benefit. For what did the Lord appoint an emblem, but for this very thing, to be observed after his death, supplying his personal presence with his spiritual image! To whomsoever, then, through the world's breadth and history, it can answer this purpose of reviving an unseen Redeemer in the mind, it belongs, as it did to the first communicants in Judæa, or as to Paul and all like him who had never seen or known Christ in the flesh.

If it be asked, why the washing of feet, as a symbol of humility, has not the same claim to perpetuity, which indeed has for it been asserted, and to some extent realized, examination and reflection might show the choice between the two rites not accidental. Not shod and guarded feet like ours in a Northern clime, but sandalled and dusty ones, were washed. Washing in its nature is a more private act than it is needful eating should be, though the washing of saints' or sinners' feet, it may be hoped, has still its place. In the washing of feet, Jesus tells his disciples to do *as* he did; in the Supper, to do over again, and often, the thing he did;—in the one case inculcating a temper only, in the other prescribing a rite. A comparison of the circumstances of the two scenes and services might confirm this view. Designing not to disparage the washing, but to defend the Supper as an ordinance, I maintain it commends itself with a strong plea to all. Only a disowning of personal relations with a Saviour, or irrational speculation in ignorance of human nature underrating the import of a symbolic influence, can make us any more than the first twelve indifferent to, however honestly we may disuse, such a rite.

But let us inquire if, beyond conventional usage or variations of personal feeling, the duration of a commemorative token may not be established on some basis of impregnable principle. Everything has its fixed date and term of life in this world. Look through the kingdoms of nature. Tribe and species, plant and tree, institution and community, last so long; nor can their existence be lengthened out artificially after the divinely fated hour. Now, in this world of human life, sentiment, and history, I maintain, symbols in a thousand forms are as real existences as the solid frame of matter itself, or as anything that grows from its bosom or lives on its sphere. What, then, is the continuance of a symbol? Its prerogative is to abide as long as the thing it is needed to signify and shadow forth. This, of course, is true of all symbols. The shield of a family or race will shine till their strength declines, and their numbers die out. Then their arms will fade and rust beyond all power to burnish their lustre, or bear on their protection or terror. The pictured eagle will appear to scream, the blazoned lion open his mouth and rear his mane, the painted lilies bloom from their delicately woven and embroidered ground, and the stars sparkle on the banners of nations, while the nations wax in might, spread their policy, expand their territory, or shake the planet they inhabit with their tread. Why should not their flags float over land and sea, fort and tower, harbor and town, long as they have a name and place and force to live among the swarming populations of men?

Let dogmas and speculations and schools of opinion come and go; so it is their nature to rise and flourish and pass; but no merely intellectual revolutions can alter or overset what has the Divine claim of reality and fact. Could the American traveller, who, seeing his country's flag displayed from a little boat on the river Rhine, felt the tears rush to his eyes, have explained his effusion, save as arising from a token of the wide-spread and lasting power of his native land?

When, however, in that war with time and nature from which nothing mortal is discharged till it succumbs, the principles and powers surrender, retreat, and decay, then the symbol must go with the antiquated, superannuated things symbolized. Then let all the fine pictures and suggestive engravings be like faint sketches and perishable drawings growing pale in the sun, as in the unmeasured existence of mankind so many significant colors have been already struck, wrapped together, and laid away to rot. But not before! reason orders, the heart cries, Not before! So be it with the symbols of our religion, — especially with this precious, chosen one of the Supper of our Lord. We will put this on the same ground with all celebrations of any other right sentiment of human nature, asking for it no favors, but only the justice that is its due. We will entreat no moment's factitious existence of the form beyond the substance, of self-sacrifice and love unto death, it displays. Let no bread be broken or wine poured on the table after his broken body and flowing blood have lost their glorious sense. But lost it yet they have not! No scenery of terrestrial events has kept so great a meaning so long; none promises coeval significance through the measureless track mankind is still to tread. What emblem that binds men in any other association together, what banner that flouts the gale in either hemisphere, or signal that dallies with any far-off ocean's breeze, can vie with the hope of this standard? Would we tear it away and blot its period? Let us then be not capricious, but consistent, and make, while we are about it, thorough work. Let us declare it nothing but folly in the world's history for picturesque symbols graven on scutcheons and shields to have silently for millions taken the place of what floods of noisy speech! Let us brand it as absurdity for the heroic Kane to have left his banner blowing in the wintry Arctic solitude at every blast from the frozen pole! Let us lower every waving fold of patriotic signification, erase from the calendar our anniversaries, of December, June, or July, and abolish every friendly, fraternal, domestic token! An ordinance that has secured its own prolongation, and looks forth to the future so sublimely from its historic mount of near two thousand years, against any man's critical negations or practical neglect, I must aver, was meant to be perpetual, and is perpetuated by God. Therefore its open invitation is not absolute, but remains.

This symbolic meaning of the table affords, moreover, a reply to the argument against the service on account of the alteration of its original style. At the outset, it may be said, it was a real supper, like the Jewish Passover, which it extended into new interpretation. It was like that eating together of the bread and salt, or drinking of the cup of water or wine, which, in tribes barbarous or civilized, has been the universal, everlasting sign of amity and good-will to every stranger or wayfarer admitted to the board. But this hearty character of its hospitality and good cheer has utterly failed. Its bits of bread, its touches and tastings of the lips, may be considered a mere apparition of eating and drinking, a hollow, unsubstantial ceremony. It often looks now like a kind of spectre. It is like the fancied return of spirits in our day, in guise of intellectual demonstration infinitely inferior, as many will say, to that of the former mortals in the flesh whose present impersonation is alleged. The scattered, silent, individual, gray communicants, that so thinly, without ardor, magnetic enthusiasm of personal communication, or mutual converse, sit apart in churches deserted of most of their common worshippers, casting from their faces a sort of ghostly light on the table and its vessels borne about, — how different from the devoted company that, putting off their dusty shoes, lay in each other's bosoms, and for the support of wearied nature abundantly partook of what was set before them!

Admitting such of the defects here stated as it would enter into my design to relieve, to the cavil also suggested I rejoin, it was by no means the satisfaction of natural hunger and thirst, that in the first instance constituted the Lord's Supper. Rather, in the midst of the feast, Jesus took bread, and gave the blessed broken loaf, and passed the cup, as omens of the bloody sacrifice of himself at hand. Were they received and consumed for so much bodily food and stimulus? Never, but purely for the soul! Are we not right to dispose of no drop or particle of the consecrated elements for the sake of the flesh, but take the nutriment and enlivening into the circulations of the heart? Yea, saith every soul that has felt their peculiar influence. The table stands not at any visible altar alone. It is spread in our imagination also. Perpetually the sacred vessels shine there. There quietly in musing hours the loaf is broken and the wine is poured, while silent around in imagination's chambers sit the loving and beloved guests.

Let the Supper be all symbol, food for thought and food for feeling, a real presence, not as the Romanist fancies of Christ's body, — what care we for that? — but of his immortal nature to immortalize ours! As, in rude sheds on mountain-sides and along lonely vales, the cross of Christ symbolizes his self-sacrifice to every passer-by, so let the table invite and welcome all who will approach. As the Scripture record may be read by all, so let this ritual pictorial language be perused. As a painting of the Last Supper, by Leonardo da Vinci, or any master, may be beheld by every eye, so be it with the actual board in the sanctuary. It is all symbol, and symbol for all whom symbol can touch. As well keep the canvas of Rubens or Volterra portraying our Lord's descent from the tree, out of sight, instead of making it the wonder and inspiration of the world, as hide the feast which prepared the sufferer for his doom.

We do not make believe eat and drink in the Supper. How many are the actual instances, in other relations of our human life, of reducing outward and material qualities to a symbolic sense! A printed line chosen out of its connection, and turned into a motto, a piece of cloth streaming at mast-head, and torn into a rag in the tempest of battle, a title or a badge for any literary or mechanical craft, a peculiar pressure of recognition in some brotherhood, a wooden ball rolled through the land to bespeak the political revolution it does something to produce, — these and a thousand things beside are so changed, and by some alchemy of sentiment reduced. What means that sound of artillery? Is there war in the territory, — troops landed, the enemies' fire opening, and we summoned to meet them? Surely for this their brazen tubes were bored or iron length cast! Do those pennons lure us to the fight? No, — the grim mouths with their deathly blaze, those meteors that flutter in the air red as the blood whose spilling they portend, that resounding alarum of the bell that martial music, and those incomparable bands of soldiery parading our streets, so far from the fear and clangor of conflict, are altered into but exulting symbols of peace Sceptic, that smilest at religion, and pretend est to overflowing patriotism, defend or deliver thyself from thy self-contradiction, ay, even the denial of what is best in thy own nature! Man of science, that canst see a natural law, but despisest a supernatural influence or fact, thy peers in intellect have apology and argument deep as any matter of thy observation for their confessing of divinity!

What is the use now of that little enclosure of Bunker-Hill, once the scene of carnage? The same again as at the creative commencement of things? Ages by-gone, before the shock of arms, it may have served some end in cultivation, or for the cattle that browsed amid the grass. But no man shall till those roods any more. No flocks on that green sward shall again find pasturage. Never, please God, to military occupation, with the dreadful science of gunnery, shall it return. It is all symbol now, — a lot in which not corn and wheat, but friendship and patriotism, may grow. Wherefore does the stone building in the centre stand? Who dwells there by day or lodges by night? What merchandise within those sightly portals and solid walls? Of what machines or stuffs of precious texture does that lofty shaft, like other tall neighboring chimneys, denote the factory? Of what iron road do those firm gates mark the station? Nothing of this: earth, granite, girded space, all is symbol! No tenants but spirits, and such as go to meet them hovering in the air! Ye, who scorn and set aside all the expressive appeals and tokens of a Christian faith, of course also care nothing for spot or monument, appointed celebration or annual day, and with hand or voice, when you have journeyed to the mount of bloody sacrifice, greet no sympathetic friend or fellow-citizen there! Not so, exclaim all. We recognize our fathers in a pure symbol! So, pure symbol is the table of the Lord. Shall the blood of countrymen be commemorated on the hill where they fell? There was a sacrifice, on another hill of Calvary, which redeemed the race and gave freedom to the earth!

In fine, shall we not conclude, our religion is not truth for the intellect or command for the conscience alone, but symbol for the soul. It is impossible for any one, who denies this principle, to make his own conduct congruous. He cannot rise in the morning, see his kindred, sit at meat, pass through the town, stop at any threshold, or enter into any relation of life, without obeying the prompting which we ask should also in the emblems of the Gospel be allowed. The very members of his body, what rises and falls with his heart-throbs, the walls of his house, the letters from his hand, the most precious stores of his privacy, by written signs and fresh or antique figures attesting what has touched him most deeply and is still dearest to his soul, are his refutation. If the savage warriors of a thousand tribes have spared as sacred the life of those that have eaten at their board, there may be some virtue of grace and love for those that eat and drink together as disciples of the Lord and followers of the Captain of their salvation.

Free grace, in short, as much as free will, fashions the sons of God. As air no less than exercise contributes to bodily health, so inspired and inspiring, as well as moral, is the perfect man. As the passive verb is an indispensable part of human speech, so the receptive temper is part of human excellence. Every influence of art, every appeal of nature, every object or event that stirs a sentiment in the human bosom, and each breath of the Holy Spirit of God, comes in proof of our dependence for character, not on direct effort alone, but a thousand involuntary impressions. By sail or carriage or balloon, as well as direct motion of the feet, one is moved. Does not sacred music, as surely as sober advice, reach the springs of conduct? Are we not astir at the holy thunder of countless voices in some grand chorus of the Elijah or Messiah, as strongly as by any cool didactic treatise? But argument is a drug and superfluity for what stands of itself, and shines in its own light. Form or symbol in religion? Dedicated building and Sabbath day themselves are part of it! I lately waited listening to the bell as it rang and tolled the people to church: stroke after stroke, quick and lively, in chiming tones, while the city's hundred belfries made response; then solemn, single, more slow, till the sound stopped altogether.

"Hark! hark! it seems to say,
As melt those sounds away,
So earth's best joys decay!
For thy life is ending!"

If a worldly man or a studious critic will object, that on technical, sectarian, or superstitious conditions such an influence depends, let him try the principle within the sphere of his own susceptibilities. Let him leave the atmosphere of his meditation or business, go to the place where he was born, roam the fields his childhood played in, enter the shadows of the hill-sides in whose coolness he lay down, or stand on the rocky points of prospect he ascended. Will he own no instruction additional to the results of his most prudent research or sharpest reasoning? He sits beside the little brook which washed his feet scores of years ago. Just as then it tinkles by him, a weak rivulet which his finger can almost fathom, and it might seem one motion of his hand could turn from its course. It tinkles and glides, and keeps its old, slender channel. But where are the children that sat beside him and sported in its sound? Where are the men that strode over the brook on their affairs, to plant or build or sail, and, as he remembers, so unlike him, heeded it not? All swept away by the vast tide of mortality, or scattered on the tossing billows of change! The generations of men and the hosts of heaven have changed their places, yet unconcernedly the little brook tinkles on as it did. Is it unworthy, then, of an intellectual being, that the stream, in its tiny flow expressing the passage of time, should signify it more vividly and truly than the formal registers of clerks, annals of historians, or all the mathematical instruments and calculations ever invented by human wit? Truly, to all, not sunk in brute sensuality, Nature has her symbols! Surely it is not unnatural, or, in the light of common sense, illegitimate, that Religion should have hers; and if she have them, like Nature, let her preserve them throughout all generations, make them coeval with her own life, and extend them without exception to the children of men!

CHAPTER V.

PROFESSION.

Many object to open communion as perverting the Supper from its use to individuals as a special profession of religion. It is enough to say in reply to this, Christ put the institution on no such ground of a profession or first acknowledgment of him, but of a commemoration by those already his disciples. They observed it as one of many indications of loyalty, free, like all other exercises and symbols, to those united in common love of the Master. Not till ages after, upon conclusion of a customary service of instruction and worship, part of the assembly, as not belonging to the innermost circle of devotees, were dismissed with terms — *Ite, missa est* — that became a title for the Romish mass, and, in the long reach of results, issued in the Protestant benediction of sending away most of the congregation, whom a true blessing would surely rather keep at the table. Well may Beranger make it the sarcastic refrain in one of his modern songs,— *Ite, missa est!* Do not the pastor in giving, and the people in receiving, a dismission of part of the congregation, enact together an untrue and unchristian division into two bodies of the whole? Blessing and dismission! Is there not something monstrous, must there not be something wrong, in such an identifying of these two things? At least I must say, and challenge one fair word of historic gainsaying, that our distinction of Church and Congregation came not from Christ or Apostles. It was a blow struck at his Body unawares, no doubt with the mistaken design of defending him,— an ill-aimed shot of ecclesiastical artillery, which, if it served any good end in that rude time, ought now, in respect to his cause, to be only reckoned as a spent ball.

But not only is there no Christian authority for identifying the Supper with a religious profession: we must beware of mistaking or over-esteeming the value of the profession itself, considered as made by individuals of one class distinguishing themselves from those of another class within the same religious body. Of nothing was Jesus more jealous than of formal and verbal professions. To say, Lord, Lord, though they did not the things he commanded, raised no persons in his regard. Whosoever cast out devils, though not in his name or outward following, he would not suffer the conceited and self-sufficient zeal of his followers to rebuke. What, then, did he mean by those words, on which hang such fear and joy, about the opposite consequences of confessing or denying him before men? Verily, it only needs to reflect what a true confession of him then was, to understand! When the ecclesiastic and civil power raised the alternative between owning the obligation of the Mosaic law, the authority of the Roman realm, or asserting allegiance to Christ in matters where his teachings conflicted with their dictates, then to confess him amid threats, in peril, beneath the scourge, before the cross,— O, that was no profession such as we commonly witness or intend! When the black looks of theological bigotry and political spite, like clouds that join before the storm, met to herald the popular hate, — when the sword that Jesus brought, sharper than any soldier's steel, cut the bonds of the nearest kindred, and the altar of sacrifice for one's self stood so often not far away for a grim termination of the scene, — it was a confession with which we can hardly presume to parallel the self-separation from our fellows amid the smiles of gratified friends and in the piping times of peace. O, that was no setting one's self apart with an air of elevation, on a scheme of safety or theory of purity, saying with the Pharisee, *I am holier than thou;* but a test, insincerity in which was made impossible by the circumstances of the case. No wonder Jesus reckoned confession of this sort at so high a rate! It meant the prison, it meant the rack, it meant disgrace, outlawry, and blood. This confession or the contrary denial should indeed have echoes from his lips in the hearing of angels, the resounding dome of heaven, and the judgment of God.

Is, then, a true confession of Christ impossible in our day? Is a confession proved worthless and false simply because, in the present state of the public mind in a nominally Christian nation, it is secure, and there is no opportunity to know whether he that makes it would rather die than take it back? Surely not. There is no objection to saying one in faith and aim is on the side of Christ, but only to his saying, by a peculiar outward demonstration, that he is more on his side than are his other followers. Moreover, there may well be opportunity, with or without verbal or ritual form, to confess him under conditions as decisive as ever. If, in circumstances any wise equivalent to those ancient ones, we own Christ for our Master; if we are true to his standard in taking a just, though unpopular course, for which we are persecuted in the community by the powers that be, which draws upon us the reproach of companions, or that general howl of the day, at which only the bravest turn not pale; if we are willingly spoiled of property, or offer up reputation for any principle he reveals; if we take our life in our hand, as less precious than the least of his precepts; if, in our own soul, we choose death for a welcome, if necessary, helpmate and bride in carrying out any measure for human welfare he proclaims; if we recognize his image and God's in any poor brother or sister driven wrongfully to extremity, and cheerfully endure what man can do unto us for our humanity, — then we confess him and are his martyrs in something like his own original sense of the word, round which blazes the supreme halo of historic glory. Let examples of modesty joined with fidelity in those earlier times admonish and encourage us! Some, for not recanting, dreadfully tortured, yet escaping with life, when honor was paid them, we are told, deprecated it, saying, *We are not martyrs, but only humble confessors of Christ.*

But thus much at least must we affirm, — that is not a true and full confession of Christ which costs us nothing. Subscribing a sectarian creed; going through a conventional process; tallying with others in a religious experience, which, if true, always answers first for itself before God; dooming our fellow-creatures for honest or unavoidable difference of opinion to the vials of eternal wrath; or by conformity sheltering ourselves from such excommunication; or confessing him merely in an external rite whose substance is not in our life and soul, — is not the confession to which he referred. Let it not be thought that in any spirit of scorn I refer to empty and fruitless outward profession. Rather with the inexpressible sorrow every witness of it should feel, and not least any one whose station may bring it directly under his eye. Ah, it is a shame that any one with the least color of truth can say, I will pick out as many good Christian men in a given religious community from those not professors as from those who are! It is a shame to have it said a man cannot be trusted in a contract more for being a professor of religion. If this be indignantly denied, who of us must not admit that, if all professors in name were real followers, they would shake village and city from pollution, scare away vice and crime, and shame private fraud and civil corruption from our bor-

5

ders, in a far different style from that in which they do!

Granting that an acceptable profession of Christ may be made without a price of exposure and suffering, rarely occurring in the same form as in the martyr-age, such a profession has no identity or limit with the Lord's Supper, coincide with it whensoever it may. To cut off the right hand of every evil habit, to pluck out the right eye of every lustful desire, to crucify earthly affections when the bleeding anguish thereof is only within, is an index pointing more keenly to the mark.

But if outward profession be the indispensable thing, is it not actually made by us all? Yes, by all who are associated in the Son's name for the Father's worship. It cannot be respectfully supposed of any such, that they are such as curious Athenians merely, or Sadducaic sceptics. Such an imputation they would have a right to resent and contradict as nothing less than a charge upon them of actual deceit; and the consciousness in any one of such a character cannot exist w thout his shamefully, with burning heat of soul, if not a blushing cheek, feeling also that his signs of faith and devotion are a wretched sham, and most unworthy pretext. Yes, we are all professors in the general, if in no self-righteous or invidious way.

We may not make peculiar professions, by which one of us distinguishes himself from another. But Jesus prescribed and for himself made none of that kind; for, when he called himself meek and lowly of heart, according to the proud, prevailing Roman standard, that was profession of ignominy rather than glory, and claim not of virtue, but reputed vice. Who of us, in his temper, can make a peculiar profession even of loving Christ more than our neighbor does? But common professions in all our Christian words, acts, services, we make. A man, asked if he belongs to the Church, answers, No! He has been to church from his childhood. Nothing in the Bible he may not have read or heard; nothing in the Hymn-book but may have been his song; every truth of preaching has been a proclamation for him; on every sentiment of prayer his soul may have ascended as with the breath of the Holy Ghost. Nay, every domestic service of religion in wedding-gladness, baptismal offerings, funeral grief, ministers of Christ may have rendered in his dwelling, — and he himself would indignantly resist any implication that closet or fireside devotion could by him be forgot. Yet he does not belong to the Church! What does he mean? That he does not join in celebrating a particular ordinance or feast! I venture to submit this is not Christ's definition. It is absurdity, superstition, a violation in words of sober fact, a denial of manifest Christian position, and it may be fatal attempt at evading obligations equally binding on all. Only evil can be the effect on the majority of a religious society, to feel and be allowed to feel they do not belong to the Church of Christ.

If this position seems like that of a cable and windlass straining unaffectedly diffident or confessedly worldly or actually unbelieving persons up to a point they in all honesty must decline to touch, then truly we must go back to first principles, and inquire for what ends we unite in building and dedicating, possessing and frequenting, houses called churches and courts of God. Men of the world talk of hypocrisy. What greater hypocrisy than to frequent a Christian sanctuary, own the edifice, choose and support the ministry, yet inwardly disown church-membership, that is, disown Christianity! — for, if we mean by Christianity anything more than a dead record of ancient words and facts, if we mean by it a living power in the world, it can be nothing but a union of human beings in love and fealty to the common Master. Shall we hold out the signal of such union, and abnegate the substance? There could be no greater nonsense to affront the human understanding, folly for angels to smile at, falsehood for God to visit and avenge! We do belong to the Church. We cannot discard or be rid of the relation. It is behind our will, in our blood and nurture. Concerning this one thing, it is too late for us to choose. Those that have come out, as they think, from the Church, have not come out of it more than of their mother's milk.

Thinkers may speculate upon one or another point, change opinions, enlarge their ideas; but the principle of life, however in words disallowed, they cannot in fact expel. The lines of the Church gird us all in, the laws of the Church bind us all up, the mercies and consolations of the Church cover us all over. Blessed to be thus embraced and included; cursed to be left out as mere worldlings, curious listeners, cold spectators! Life and death, joy and sorrow, voices of the past, hushed on earthly lips, and turned into calls from heaven, are vouchers of our connection. We dare not, if we could, take our place outside. Our antecedents are in us irrevocably and for ever. We shall allow none to put us out, more or less advanced as Christians though we be. More than once has the statesman, from some cause, under a cloud with his party, been heard to exclaim, — *Who will put me out?* Who, that loves and follows Jesus Christ, may not with humble boldness and inflexible meekness say the same! Even the doubter in crowded street or philosophic hermitage is affected by the

Gospel he criticises, and, as a partial thing, would reject.

The very nature of the Church confirms our whole argument. The body ecclesiastic is an organism like the body politic. There are better and poorer citizens: but citizens all born or naturalized Americans are. There is a naturalizing in the Church. Every babe of Christian parents is by nature a commencing, by continuing grace a perfect Christian. But, we are asked, is there not in every true soul's history a moment of regeneration, which should be signalized by coming to the table? and is not this a profession appropriate to be made? Far be it from me to think lightly of any epoch whatsoever in the spiritual life! When the soul, offspring of God, first is made sensible of its relation to him, and, conscious of an Almighty parentage, says, *Henceforth I will call no man father upon earth;* when, knowing the weakness and sorrow that waylay the pilgrim in time, it sees a Saviour in Jesus Christ, the Son of God; when it resolves to trust its fortunes for ever to the Divine Spirit and Word, — then some attestation of its purpose may become it well. No formal attestation alone, or chiefly, should it regard. Yet the simple and beautiful ordinance of the Supper may meet and feed those feelings of love continually, otherwise in holy working exercised and expressed. But, however much may be made of this particular expression in such a view of a religious life, desirable as parents may hold it that their children should have in this ceremony something, while their religious nature unfolds, to look forward to, — as indeed not seldom old men are known to contemplate its observance before they die, — the principle I advocate, instead of being surrendered, is only the more heightened and advanced. Instead of being for prospective ends deprived of this ordinance, how much better opportunity for its profitable use will the young enjoy for having been brought up in its presence, than if from childhood excluded, like heathens, from its sight! Like the rising light, according to the old dispensation, like the growing corn, according to the new, without noisy break, showy observation, or ostentatious profession, will their progress thus be. Not at church-meetings or before ecclesiastical officers alone, but in every deed of the hands and articulation of the lips, will the profession of Christ appear.

I cannot help being persuaded that this long training from the first, by opening to eye and ear and heart of all every method of Christian instruction and growth, though no chronic disease or radical evil of this world can be suddenly banished or cured, will make religion more cordial and stable on earth. Churchman and theologian are pained to hear it said of some one, *He was a good man, though no professor of religion;* but, while so many a professor and preacher falls below the manifesto of faith, they must not be surprised. Is not this just what the centurion meant to say of Jesus as he expired: This was a good man, Son of God, though no professor in the Jewish Church? Disconnected from lowly goodness, in the very phrase *profession of religion*, as a peculiarity of one believer among or within the circle of others, to every generous mind, there will always be some sense of disgust. It is not a phrase of Christ or of Scripture, separate from the life. To profess to have more love, faith, purity, than others, under the common Christian standard, is like an artisan professing to be the most skilful of his craft, a scholar the most learned in his department, a painter, poet, intellectual or spiritual worker of any sort, the most accomplished of his guild. Where is most true religion, beauty of holiness, and fervor of affection, it will be most acted and least peculiarly professed. But a common symbol, open to all, can have in it no egotism of sanctimony. It would broadly fold the world.

Upon the whole subject of profession, no system more than the Congregational, as at present administered, is open to critical remark. It regards partaking of the Supper as the note of a peculiar religious experience. But the initiatory rite of baptism, by which one is supposed to enter the Church, it confers not only on babes, but very widely upon all children presented for it, whether of church-members or non-communicants and unbaptized. The charge herein made upon it, of inconsistency, cannot well be set aside. Its ecclesiasticism is confused. Its footing is uncertain. It cannot stay where it is, but must go either backward or forward. Forward let it go! Forward it will go, and the retrospect of its course, as of the successive geologic ages, will show even the incongruous mixtures of opposite elements as but part of the way to solid simplicity and crystalline clearness in the truth of Christ.

CHAPTER VI.

BAPTISM.

It may be considered a fatal argument against open communion of the Lord's Supper, that the unbaptized may come to the table. The Christian claim, the spiritual beauty, the proper or expedient priority in order of the rite of baptism being admitted, yet for its precedence in every possible case there is no absolute authority. Christ, Apostles, the Bible, nowhere can be quoted in final settlement of this point. In one instance, baptism is named after drinking of the cup. In short, we have no Christian right to refuse the elements to such as sincerely and spiritually desire to receive them, simply because they have not been baptized. Both the ordinances, unessential in themselves, are emblems of essential things, love and purity together making the life of the

Gospel, although one may be a communicant in the Church and not a real member, or baptized and not purified.

While there is no rigid injunction of Scripture or ultimate decree of reason on their chronological succession, the ordinances must be observed according to the spiritual motions of individual souls, or both the grand feelings of the human breast, elements of religion and attributes of God, as not seldom has been the case, may be signified in the same hour of solemn joy at the same altar of praise and prayer; and certainly a doubt respecting the rite of baptism or the fit mode of its administration should not exclude for ever a loving soul from the table, unless we will make it the table of a sect, not of the Lord.

Technical interpretations have been made of baptism, as expressive, not of inward purity, but of party spirit and a theological creed. Thus, in contradiction of the "one baptism" Paul asserts in connection with the other glorious unities of the Christian faith, every sect has had its own, significant of its own peculiarities of theological belief.

But history shows, — as the water itself from sea and cloud, river and spring, would testify, — that the original idea of a rite which began in the most ancient lustrations of the world, passed from Gentilism to Judaism, and from the Hebrew to the Christian, was of moral purity; and in proportion as the practice of the Church has kept this idea uppermost in lively application to the consciences of men, has the rite been effective, according to the strong intimation of John the Baptist, when he said, though he had baptized with water, his mightier successor should baptize with the Holy Ghost and with fire. This thought alone covers the whole ground, from childish innocence to manly and divine sanctification. The adventitious idea of baptism as a token of doctrinal soundness for admission to some denominational circle, how different from that of the time when, robed in white, significant of purity, the candidate approached the font or stood under the sprinkled drops while the Holy Spirit was represented hovering over the neophyte till he emerged innocent as from a lustration of the soul! The act was not purity itself, as ecclesiastical superstition has since made it, but the sign of purity; as Augustine says, the sacraments are not the things, but only their tokens.

If it be said baptism was conversion regeneration, or universally a sign thereof, the question arises, Was it so in regard to Jesus Christ? Did he, unspotted Lamb of God, need to turn or be born again? No, — baptism is an emblem, whether connected with and coming before or after any other emblem or not. In fact, it no doubt very early came before. The promise being, as Peter said, to the men of Israel and their children, whole households, as of the jailer and of Stephanas, were baptized, including, doubtless, those of tender age, if the families were like ours, and not rare or anomalous cases of childless connections, hardly namable as families in any ancient or modern sense. If such barren households alone had been contemplated in the reference, and it were also vitally important that no offspring of a tender age should receive the rite, it is inconceivable all hint or warning of facts so momentous should have been withheld. When that pearl of our nature's purity, so easily lost, had dropped in the muddy ways of the world, baptism was still symbolic of purity not possessed, but by God's grace and Christ's influence to be regained or won in a quality more precious than any childish inoffensiveness, which never reaches the full idea of holiness unto the Lord. Truly purity in the Divine sense is no merely native and negative quality, but a positive grace. The *purified* are the pure. Sanctification through truth and discipline is the mark of the saved. Therefore by a fine and just instinct are they called *saints*, or persons made holy. Good cause is there why the manner of the ordinance cannot be precisely fixed, the Holy Spirit having matters of more importance than to decide, in favor of any disputant, our senseless external controversies of plunging, pouring, or sprinkling.

But, disowning all exercise of despoti

judgment, the precedence of the Supper by baptism, and the custom of infant baptism, as a point, if not of supreme obligation, yet of ecclesiastical decorum, may be maintained, not only on the basis of the ancient record, of the mind of Christ, of wide-spread use in subsequent ages, and of the present method of the immense majority of the Church, but of the emblematic signification of the service. I allege the authority of reason in the absence of that of Holy Writ. If it meant conversion at the outset, as the religion entered into the generations of mankind, this meaning could not last, for demonstrably the children of Christian parents were expected to become Christians, not in the original way of taking the kingdom of God by violence, but in that of growth and training. So Jesus intended in saying that of such as little children was his kingdom, and directing that all nations, without distinction of age, should be baptized. So Paul signified, tracing Timothy's faith to his mother, Eunice, and grandmother, Lois. Such is the Apostle's language, again, of bringing up children in the nurture and admonition of the Lord. The mode of making verbal and textual arguments against this is a killing of the spirit with the letter, and setting grammar and lexicon above the genius of the compositions they should expound.

Least of all in religion should we forget that hereditary law, which, whether we remember it or not, is mighty in all the relations and processes of our life. Just as Americans born become citizens of this country, not, like foreigners, by being formally naturalized, but insensibly inspired with the quality of our free institutions, so the children of Christendom should become Christians, not by conversion, but by education, — Christianity, like the policy of our constitution and laws, being a working power upon and within them from their birth. As Franklin says he was a reader from his infancy, so they should be learners in the school of Christ.

I know the wide contradiction of this view. On the theory of total depravity, all are born and remain utterly remote from

God, perfect heathens, till a sudden influence strikes one or another individual midway in life, or, like a spiritual tornado, sweeps a host at once into the kingdom. No theory of human nature could be more gross. It is one of those cases where we despair of reasoning, not because the arguments are so few, but so many we can scarce without weariness get through adducing them, and because we may be hopeless of touching one who upon such a question, where the matter is so obvious, needs any argument at all. But the truth of the general scheme I must utterly deny. It is hard to tell to which it runs most counter, Scripture, reason, or fact. It represents the human race, not as a living, concrete thing, but a mere aggregate of disintegrated particles, a heap of sand whose grains lie mechanically without coherence together. Such we know it is not. Mankind is not, and never has been, a mass of unconnected, identically equal individualities. There is a family and national character, a social as well as personal unity. As in Adam all die, in Christ all are made alive. The variety God loves in all his works appears most of all in humanity. All childhood is not the same, more than all flesh, of any kind, or all bodies terrestrial or celestial, are the same. Into every child of a day old enter a thousand component parts, — far-off ancestry, immediate parentage, untraceable impressions, the mutual fitness and fidelity of those whose offspring it becomes, — all fusing into marvellous oneness, wonderfully to give it constitutional peculiarity all its own. When, as has not seldom happened in the world's history, in the very cradle one babe is treacherously and feloniously substituted for another, well is it called *a changeling!* It is not and cannot be the same; for babes — O fact of tremendous import we have so little considered! — babes differ as much as men and women.

Science and religion, with united appeal, certify us it is time indeed to dismiss our hasty and foolish doctrine, which stands so injuriously in the way of all intelligent individual culture, that human beings when they are born are either so many sheets of pure white paper or so many manuscripts alike utterly blotted and foul. In the very beginnings of human life, from the progeny of the poor Hottentot and hunted Bushman to the loftiest type civilization and Christianity can produce, how immense that scale of diversity, for which God will justify himself, as for making one of his creatures an angel and another a worm! The Christian is not the Pagan kind or stock; but babe differs from babe as animal from animal and plant from plant. Persons sometimes adopt children on the supposition of all originally being fac-simile copies of each other, and every following year of life only evinces the terrible mistake. Not unmeaning is the Scripture in its thousand positive and negative statements: "The generation of the upright shall be blessed." Truly I know of no sentence more fearful in the implications of warning the very glory of its meaning and promise involves! With the direct proposition rolls in the converse, as the other wheel of the shining and terrible chariot of God. What a motive to uprightness to bless our posterity! What a solemn color on the ardor of early love in wedded ties! What a thunderbolt from the heavens on all impurity and discord! What a benediction of Heaven on harmonious and unblemished souls! When arrive the new beings, little voyagers from the everlasting shore, with the most precious freight for this temporary harbor of earth, in what awful aspect, only by the mingling lustre of holiest affection made cheerful to our thought, arises the obligation by word and deed to lead them to truth and virtue! Ah, how great is the proportion of manhood and womanhood, created for such oneness, that has really pondered this essential verity? How many of those youth, that lead in the new over the graves of the older race, for a fresh pilgrimage through earth toward a hoped-for everlasting rest, are taking it to heart as they should? Let them beware lest the light become the lightning of God!

To such as are persuaded of doctrines by particular passages urged in their support, the local argument might be brought with irresistible weight in proof that it is the object of Christ so to hallow human relations, that, when our children are born, they should be born into the Divine kingdom, the second birth not displacing but concurring with the first, the natural and spiritual not opposed but flowing together. Not verily to destroy or thrust aside, but to take up and redeem out of all perishing the natural, is the spiritual influence sent. That, in fact, the life of nature is often carnal, passionate, and worldly from the creative starting even into adult years, — so that the methed of alarm, awakening, and revival must go along with the process of nurture, as, for the bodily life and health of human beings, medicine mixes or alternates with food, — it is certainly impossible to deny. But as the aim, and to a good degree the result, in social advancement, by better diet and exercise, is to dispense with medicine, diminish its doses, and dwarf its pills, till, in some millennial day of physical regeneration, it shall disappear altogether, so should we try to substitute the soul's true activity and nourishment for the treatment of its morbid states. Ay, for theological drugs that heal by poisoning, and the bedridden sloth, which at best is a substitute of doing nothing instead of doing ill, let the spirit at last have wholesome motion and food. Nay, as for disease itself kindly nursing is often the most effectual cure, so in the provisions and exercises of God's house should be found the best remedy for the various sickness of sin.

When, in any considerable measure, shall appear that chosen generation and peculiar people described and predicted in the word of truth; when the blessed heritage, promised to our seed and seed's seed after us, shall come; when that manifestation of the sons of God, the whole creation travaileth and groaneth for, shall be made, — all that is meant by the "one baptism" and the Lord's table shall be seen to be the pure bond of humanity in him. For that sublime moral beauty let us rejoice to suffer and toil.

I stood on Boston Common, at twilight waxing into darkness, as the day of our great national anniversary last passed away. A hundred thousand people stood there quiet with one feeling and faces turned all one way. A shudder of joy passed over me at the union of such a host, even for an end so trivial as an hour's sport. But thoughts other than of the passing recreation instantly from the broad spectacle forced their way. Little gazed I at the novel, magnificent fire-works, they charmed the eye so much less than that sight of an army, greater perhaps than ever at once actually in conflict of battle, met peacefully to witness them. The streaming and flashing lights, amid whose blaze and explosion I was, were but candles for me to survey the living scene of humanity, grander I will not say than the pyrotechnic display, but than Alps or seas or stars. If the union of men for a purpose so transient and superficial can be so inspiring and impressive to the mind, what would be the effect of their perfect oneness for the great cause of religion, the honor of God, the likeness of Christ, the saving of the human soul! That would fulfil the end of all rituals indeed. That would be a baptism, not of John, but of the Holy Ghost and of fire.

CHAPTER VII.

DISCIPLINE.

One of the arguments principally relied on for the partial and exclusive administration of the Lord's Supper is its value in the discipline of the Church. This value is thought to be threefold, — in the strict terms of faith and character prescribed for admission to it, in a specifying of the heresies or faults for which one may be excommunicated or expelled, and in an implication of the perilous or lost condition of the general body that have not yet accepted the ecclesiastic offers of salvation, nor been enrolled as members among the elect. This disciplinary authority is maintained by what in the Romish system is regarded as veritably one of the seven sacraments, namely, the "Orders" or persons in official rank. But, I must reply, Christ himself, in speaking of his Church, which he would build on "this rock," never appointed any hierarchy at all. On the contrary, he so warned his disciples against being called Rabbi, or being anything but each other's servants, that even the modern titles of honor among religious persons, such as Reverend, with their various aggravations of phrase, though endured as convenient designations of classes and persons, or defended as marks of respect for learning and character from honorable bodies, seem scarce compatible with moral dignity, or consistent with the Master's wish. In a better day such rewards of excellence will be disused, and the technical authority to sentence or punish now lodged in ecclesiastical officers, will be lost in that universal brotherhood of which the Lord himself is head.

It may, however, be rejoined, that, in his earthly days, with his few disciples, or in the times immediately succeeding his death and resurrection, when his followers were kept together by persecution, and their suffering from others was indeed discipline enough, they needed from one another only comfort and good cheer; but when they multiplied and differed among themselves, a severe organization, with laws, pains, and penalties, was indispensable. It would lead me too far to go now into the general subject of ecclesiastical rule and power. Briefly, then, whatever discipline in the Church may be necessary, I shall only maintain here that the Lord's Supper cannot properly be made an instrument of such discipline.

It will not be pretended that Jesus himself ever made his table such an instrument, or gave one hint of its becoming such. This was not because he overlooked the liabilities of social transgression and trouble among his adherents, or pleased himself with any dream of perpetual peace and concord. In case of an offence between brethren, he enjoins first conference between themselves privately, then an explanation in the presence of witnesses, and afterwards a communication to the Church; in case of all which steps being successively ineffectual, he recommends conscientious coldness and moral aversion as for a while the best treatment for the obstinate offender, specifying, however, no measure of positive infliction or voted dismissal. But he never put, nor I think can be conceived of as allowing others to put, the tenderest token of his own love to such a purpose, or rather abuse. He never authorized separation from that as retribution, though voluntary going out from it, as at first, might be the consequence of guilt.

Let me not be misunderstood as objecting to discipline, or the idea of it, altogether. In the Apostolic Church it seems to have been sometimes needful. But the painful excision of a member from the whole body, after the Apostolic example, which extreme circumstances may justify, is better than to employ the Supper for correction, as, in the society of the world, men are punished by not being invited to a feast. Even those among the Corinthians who turned the sacred meal into a scene of gluttony and drunkenness, were not forbidden again to celebrate it, but commanded to examine themselves, and told they were eating and drinking their own condemnation.

But reflect how the existing supposition is

one of amazement and affront! Of a congregation, decently wonted, perhaps for ages in one place, to all other teachings and influences of our holy faith, the larger part, for omitting some prescribed process, or failing to approach through some particular avenue, whose gate and lock are under the minister's hand, shall only be permitted to gaze at the uncovered, shining vessels, and then go, leaving a little minority to this certainly most exclusive of all festival ceremonies, presence at which is the Christian honor, and its abandonment religious disgrace! A heathen or savage barbarian might fitly be required to understand the ordinance before approaching it. But has not line upon line, generation after generation in our churches, sufficed to indoctrinate all of us? Certain conditions in every voluntary association it may be necessary to lay down. But, among all profanations, none can be more gross than to degrade the Lord's Supper into a rod. To deprive a rebellious child of his food is not thought very judicious, though with some a common punishment. Still worse is it to take away, in any form, the bread of life from the soul. What! discipline a man by robbing him of the very means of grace? Shall we apply this to other means in religion? Would we discipline one by shutting up from him, as Rome does, the Scriptures, locking the door of his closet, or making the Sunday, that common privilege, shine no Sabbath day for him?

We put a Bible in the prisoner's cell: the Sabbath day, that dawns for the rest of the world, releases the poor convicts from the heavy tools in their toilsome yard; and the pious with their prayers seek to win the lunatics, crazed by misfortune or sin, back from their wanderings in the weary, labyrinthine ways of unreason. Shall there be, then, a means of religion which we deny to whosoever stands on the broad, Christian platform, or for any man, however unworthy, turn into a rack and a whip? If we discipline no man by deprivation of the common means of grace, why discipline him by denying to him that other institution, which He who commanded to enter the closet, whose life makes the best part of the Bible, and whose resurrection fixed the observance of Sunday, added for the spiritual training of mankind? No, discipline him by refuting his errors, laying a ban of disapprobation on his folly and vice, or by withdrawing your confidence from his indiscretion, but not by excluding him from the Lord's table, whose emblems of unearthly goodness and love to the end may recall him to a better mind. Discipline him by rebuke and by expostulation, not by such disunion. Use other things,—the denunciations of Holy Writ on the wicked, portentous foretellings of their fate, — use sharpness and warning, frowning and distrust; but spare this blessed ordinance, — weave it not into a lash of torture, gentle and gracious in its own nature and substance as it is! Such Christ meant it not to be when he instituted it before the scourge was laid on himself, or the crown of thorns platted for his own temples.

But rarely, in a well-constituted Church, can the harsher modes of discipline mentioned be requisite. Recently, — if I may cover a particular case with a kindly and respectful generality, — an instance of discipline was related to me as in triumphant proof of strict ecclesiastical organization and partial administration of the Lord's Supper. But how was the gross offender actually dealt with? By private expulsion or a public brand given over to all evil? No, but sought by the best love and persuasion of the Church, kept within the lines, under the great earthly mother's wings, fed still at her board, and from perdition saved! *I will pursue that man, I will never give him up*, said a great preacher of a wasted and profligate gambler he had described; and, as he said it, the sweat mingled with tears on his burning cheeks. That was the very spirit of the Lord!

It has been said, every true circle of human beings gathered by a real principle of association, will protect itself. How true this is of the Church we may learn from that Apostolic language, — "They went out from us because they were not of us; for had they been of us, they would, no doubt, have continued with us." In a glorious and spotless Church, what incorrigibly bad man would desire to be united? What is such a Church but a disinterested, benevolent, self-denying company, engaged in labors of mercy and all good works? How can the mean, impure, selfish, wish to be of it? It is no band of self-glorifying persons, taking care of their own reputation, securing to themselves a monopoly or lion's share of the good things of this life, that self-seekers should yearn for the prerogatives of their company! If it become such, and thus afford cause for the low-minded, worldly-ambitious, and vain to covet its intercourse, and a share in the spoils, it is no longer of Christ's Church. Verily, if it be a true Church, they will not and cannot be in it to be driven out, any more than they could or would be in heaven, calling for angels to be officers of justice for their expulsion thence.

With his own heaven or hell moves every man, as with its atmosphere the earth. No creature will breathe or live out of its own element. Misers will not be likely to be where they are often required to put their hands in their pockets; the self-indulgent, where they must spend their time in visiting the sick and the poor; or the lovers of pleasure among those chiefly concerned for the pagan and prisoner, the oppressed and enslaved. Who has not observed that none will be teachers in a Sunday school, but those loving the young; or punctually frequent even a little sewing-circle, but such as are glad to work for the needy; or go to any sacred conference, but those fond of religious conversation and prayer? Such fellowships may well say to the whole world, *Come, all who will join our enterprise, and do as we do!*

Cases of surgery, in the imperfection of the most sanctified human nature, may arise in every social body. It may possibly be necessary to cut off persons from some imperfect, local organism of the Church. This I admit, though in my own experience not knowing the instance, and only pleading, if the instance exist, *Let not the Lord's Supper be the knife!* In proportion as any body individual or social is healthy, it will spontaneously expel every foreign substance alien to its life and injuring its best estate. In proportion as the Church anywhere is mighty, it will, to convert and absorb what is most alien to its own nature, have a power derived from the redeeming One. Not independency, but union, is the great word. Said one, in noble criticism of the ultra-Protestant radicalism and disuniting temper of our day, *I come not out, I stay within!* Verily, the necessity to drive away is a sentence not only on the driven, but those that drive.

The idea of utter exclusion from our sympathy of anything human, is, in short, not a Christian idea. The human being we are never to forsake. If the sick and sinful were the very ones on whose account the Son of God was manifested, surely our duty is hope and effort for every man. Moreover, in this matter of treating the unsound and morally diseased, have we sufficiently considered what a discipline may be found, not in wrath or hatred, but love? Ah, have we forgotten the lesson of our Lord's foremost parable of the Prodigal Son? Do we think the father's course in that case was mere doting and indulgence? No, that fatted calf did not, after all, taste so sweet to the younger son, that the elder brother need have envied him! There was more blushing than composure in the face after that best robe had been put on; the ring shining on the finger sparkled to his eyes with a rather melancholy reflection of the sun; and the prodigal's feet burned more in the very shoes brought for them, than among the sands and rocks of the desert. There was some choking in that food, and some lingering at that dance! It was the discipline of kindness, which wields a sharper sword for the human heart than cruelty ever handled. Of such discipline have we fathomed the power and measured the scale?

But of this disciplinary exclusion we are to consider the effects, not only on those removed, but those retained. If on the former the direct censure be wholesome and good, alike and equally so on the latter is the implied estimate of praise? Do we not eulogize ourselves when on moral grounds we say of anybody, he is not good enough society for us? Did Jesus ever say so of others? What society did he keep or avoid? He did not exclude even the Pharisee from his hearing and following. The Pharisee and the Pharisee's church excluded him. To be exclusive is to be pharisaic, and to confirm ourselves in the sanctimony we display. No man's opinion of his holiness is more or other than disproof of the holiness itself.

Exclusion from the Lord's Supper, being an improper discipline, has also of course been very ineffectual. God discriminates, and will have it for his prerogative for his creatures' good to divide one from another. But no net, cast into the sea of the world, has ever been able to separate the saints from the sinners to the eye and judgment of man, any more than the fisherman's net can distinguish between the good and the bad in the tenants of the briny deep. Ah, nothing is so perilous, has caused so many falls from grace, or prevented so many an attainment thereof, as private or mutual self-esteem. Moreover, the nominal and visible Church has no more than any other association the privilege of embracing only immaculate members. Nay, the unblemished have often been cast out of it, and the polluted kept; nor will the incorrupt in its circle be benefited by being among themselves so reckoned and styled.

No temples that were ever built can contain the pure in heart, no lines that were ever drawn can gird them in. If they themselves understand that they are being marked and classified, they will not stay to be counted. The only thing in this world that will not bear the fixing on itself of its own stamp, is sanctity. It runs still upon its endless errands of God's service and the good of man, hides from fame, submits to no blazonry, confesses only its short-comings, and refers itself to none but the final bar of Him who inspired and sustains it. It cannot be caught, more than his Spirit, on its way. It takes the Lord's Supper, like any other exercise, not as the end of its being, or the height of its doing, but only as grateful rest and refreshment, to pursue again that truth and righteousness which are the everlasting objects enjoined by the Master, if by means of, yet beyond all ritual forms.

If it be said discipline is involved in that text of Scripture, "Let a man examine himself, and so let him eat of that bread, and drink of that cup," it will occur to every one as a very proper exhortation in regard to those before explained Corinthian excesses of appetite, which the Apostle rebuked as an unworthy eating and drinking of condemnation to one's self, and which certainly are not repeated among us. Self-examination for the Lord's Supper, indeed! But is not self-examination a wholesome precaution and needful preparation for every other religious service? In regard to the ordinary worship of his time Jesus certainly gives a far more solemn and even fearful charge, in requiring the man who has actually brought his gift to the altar, if he remembers that his brother has aught against him, instantly to leave it and go forth that he may first be reconciled to his brother before daring to offer to God his gift. How, therefore, in the line quoted, is there any intent to discriminate, either as privilege or instrument of penalty, one act or ordinance in religion from another?

CHAPTER VIII.

DEVELOPMENT.

It is sometimes said, — Though there is no proper Christian or Apostolic authority, and no literal justification in the New Testament for making the Supper an exclusive rite, a test of character or bar of judgment to divide between the Lord's foes and his followers, yet this fact does not disallow such a use of it. For it was not possible to prescribe particulars in the administration through every age of all things in the Church. The world itself would not have contained the books necessarily written to this end. Jesus left it to his disciples to decide modes of ecclesiastical and moral action, according to their own discretion, as occasion should arise. How many of our most settled religious customs have no precise warrant in Holy Writ!

This is that theory of Development which

has played so great part in modern speculation. Rightly construed, it is a true theory. He that plants a seed is responsible, doubtless, not for the seed only, but for what it fairly grows to be. His intention reaches into the future and into the air. The oak is in the acorn; every living creature was once wrapped up in its germ, every individual rational or moral existence folded under some exact type, and every institution is but the waxing and incarnation of a principle. So our religion is not merely a sermon, parable, word, or miracle. It is not, as many suppose, a set of maxims, doctrinal abstractions, celestial revelations for the simple management of private understandings and individual self-application alone. But, according to the figures in the pages of its own books, it is a building that rises, a plant that grows, a body that waxes, a spirit that animates with pulsations ever more wide. The external form of the Gospel was not with the Apostles precisely what it was with Christ, nor, as ten thousand quotations might show, with the Fathers as with the Apostles, nor with us as with the

Fathers. Are the original methods binding on us? Does Jesus Christ himself look with displeasure on popedoms and bishoprics themselves, more than upon councils and synods? Profound and subtile, and not easily answered questions! We can only say, and must admit, that our religion is, in the concrete, whatever its original facts and words have vitally through the whole world become. Christianity, as it first appeared, was but a sowing, of which Christendom is the fruit and outgrowth.

Yet, I apprehend, however extensive may be the application of this truth to outward modes and shapes, it cannot properly be used to change in Christian ordinances the property and purpose, which are precise, and were defined and laid down at the beginning. If, for example, the Supper had in Christ's thought demonstrably a certain design of affection and common fellowship, to restrict or make it express another, especially a contrary idea of censure and division, would not develop, but pervert it altogether. It would be not the same, but a quite different rite. It would, in fact, be no longer the Lord's Supper, but the supper of a sect. The latter has no spiritual likeness, but only a material similitude to the former. There have been a great many tables of communion with which truly the Lord has had very little to do! He never sat there! As the naturalist tells us one bird sometimes uses the nest of another to hatch and rear its young, so spiritually in the annals of the Church under the cover of Christianity we know what alien broods have been brought forth, whose hate and wrath have devoured the gentle virtues of the Gospel in the rightful spot even of their own nativity.

What, then, in this matter, is the criterion by which to judge? On the true theory of development, not the intrinsic, but only the material quality, better to accommodate the truth, can fitly be altered. Thus the intention of baptism, the principle under the form may be expressed and fulfilled under any one of the external methods of its administration, sprinkling, affusion, or immersion. The purport, too, of the Lord's Supper may be equally well maintained, whatever be the size of the room, cathedral, or conventicle,—the substance of the vessels, earthen or gold,—the character of the food, or the posture at the table. But to make it the object and use of the Supper to separate between true believers, as we account them, and heretics, so called, because in modes of faith not following us,—to hold it in hand as our ruler and plummet to draw a line between supposed saints and sinners,—is to drop the Lord's proposal, and adopt, not only another, but one utterly inconsistent therewith.

No doctrine, indeed, requires more careful and conscientious handling than this of development; for none is so susceptible of misuse, or may be employed so deceptively to lead in opposite directions at once. It may serve Rome or Reason apparently almost equally well. It may be so treated as to ascribe to the Gospel whatever, in the long course of time, and the waywardness of human passions, has been foully connected with, as well as purely opened from it. It may justify the excrescence, accretion, and poisonous parasite, no less than the glorious, healthy branching out of that tree of life, whose leaves alone are for the healing of the nations. Free-thinker and pope, by dexterous logic, alike make it serve their turn. Its principal and most elaborate treatment has been in vindication of the scarlet woman's own perilous, error-comprehending assumption, which it is the very genius of Protestantism to throw off, that the Church, rather than the Book or the Spirit, is the paramount authority in our religion. It is sworn in, as own brother, with the doctrine of necessity; and, made but another shape of the dangerous teaching of optimism, goes far to abolish moral distinctions, declaring, *Whatever is, is right.*

This, of course, pertains to the theory in its wrong and abusive construction. Unquestionably from the divine original of our faith much has been developed for the very joy and honor of our being. Undoubtedly this is the test of the worth and power of anything in nature or the moral kingdom, — what, how much, and how long will be its growth? He that looks at a tiny feathery hull, one of the least pretending of living particles on the ground, feels his respect for it marvellously increased when told that from it may spring the mighty elm that will overshadow the plain. But no expansion beside is comparable to that of our faith. What is best in human character, what is grandest in human enterprise, what is holiest in human love, is all its development. Christianity, as it practically is, is nothing but development from Christianity as it originally was. Every preaching in solemn temples of its creed, every little tract containing its sense, which in these days like winged seed the colporteur scatters on all the winds that blow under heaven, and every holy embassy, more momentous than plenipotentiary political ministries, sent to savage tribes even unto the ends of the earth,—every humane cause at home for the relief of the ignorant and wretched, blind and dumb, oppressed and enslaved,—or for the diffusion of peace over this globe, more shaken in all ages with war than earthquakes,—is a development of Christianity. None of these things in their present shape existed at the birth of our religion, and most of them did not exist at all. Yet they are all the carrying out of its intention, as much as the yellow harvest is of the husbandman's planting, or as the cedars of Lebanon are of the germs which God's own hand dropped on the sacred hill-side, and whose sprouting with the infancy of his Gospel Jesus himself possibly witnessed millenniums ago.

But the hierarchies of priestly orders that have lorded it over God's heritage, the papal infallibility, indulgences sold for sin, absolutions by human power, monkish and superstitious sunderings of the legitimate ties between man and woman under color of purity, to end in the practice of hidden and nameless sensuality, are no development of our faith. Neither are the bigotry, exclusiveness, and tyranny over the human mind, which have required new Luthers to arise since, as he had his predecessors before the Reformation, a development of the Gospel, but of that pride, selfishness, and uncharitableness of the human heart, which the Saviour was sent to root out of its very core. When we speak of development, we must consider both if the development be real and legitimate, and of what it is. Not only Christianity has been growing, but a half-sanctified human nature with and in it. Archbishop Whately's "Errors of Romanism traced to their Root in Human Nature," was surely the most just and philosophic of titles. Not only how much has grown out of, but also how much has grown over the Divine revelation! have we cause to exclaim. We sometimes see a tree folded to the very top with a vine that came forth at first as but a humble and unostentatious creeper from the ground. But the tree dwindles and withers like the mythologic hero, in the poisonous cloak of this embrace.

From a true Christian development there could be no greater departure than in the partial administration of the Lord's Supper. No severe comparisons or sharp contrasts of their respective deservings or demerits did he employ to dissolve the company of his followers as entitled or unfit for seats at his board. He extended the blessed symbols of his love and self-sacrifice to all those who had been with him, and in the spirit that would have reached them forth to everybody in the world disposed to receive them. Whom would he, that ate with publicans and sinners, not have permitted to eat with him? Against whom, that even desired to come in, would he have shut the door? Were any bars lifted at the entrance of that upper room? Alas! who in Jerusalem wanted to share the dread omen of that broken loaf, and to drink of the cup

> "that was not wine,
> But sorrow, fear, and blood"?

From whom, then, in his temper, shall it now be withheld? Nay, who of us can refuse to taste that cup of Him who tasted death for us all? or who venture to keep it back from any that desire to taste? When, in a late Diet in Sweden, it was by law made a crime to administer or receive the Lord's Supper save in the regular hierarchy, it could hardly be regarded as developing his design. What Christian, in any emergency, might not with fellow-believers celebrate the feast? To welcome all that Jesus would have welcomed, to make that feast the means of tender thought and self-devotion, to secure answers and acceptances of the invitation wide as the world, to which so greatly beyond all other teachers he appealed, — this, and no narrow hedging up of the table to a select party, develops its design.

But to vindicate close communion, with no fairness can the doctrine of development be applied. That is contraction rather; for in it the progress is less than the beginning and the unfolding, contrary to all example or analogy, — smaller than what is unfolded. Even were the acorn seen exceeding in magnitude the oak, close communion would hardly be the tree or flower of that seed of fraternal fellowship Jesus and his Apostles planted. In this matter we want properly no development at all, but only continuation of first custom. As with the telegraphic wire, the course must be completed, and the flash pass round the whole circle to the point from which it started, before the message can reach its destination, so with Christian principles and rites. In the Church we begin and end with open communion. The whole development-theory in each application must be sharply scanned, like any vegetable growth subject to blight or infested with foes. Every living thing, natural or spiritual, has its enemies, and that alone can be a true development of the Gospel, which realizes the Lord's design of making reality prevail over appearance, and substance over show, in every religious procedure or form.

CHAPTER IX.

SINCERITY.

It is objected to Open Communion, that, every bar being taken away, some may come who are not sincere; and insincerity in such a service is a deadly sin. But is it no sin, or a less sin, in matters outside of the Lord's Supper? May we be insincere in one thing more pardonably than in another? If so, then sincerity is not a constant, but an occasional virtue, of no absolute and invariable, but only a contingent obligation and importance. Unlike a tideless sea of God in the soul, it thus ebbs and flows with the hours, and on diverse shores of the world. Such sincerity is no virtue at all; for this is the definition of a virtue, that it derives its worth and consequence not from without, but from the intrinsic nature and everlasting laws of moral being.

Besides, why should the sincerity of this more than any other service be guarded with exclusive lines? The house of God is regularly opened for the most solemn exercises to human beings possible, — of prayers to Him, and songs of praise. Some may enter and engage in these insincerely. Is this a reason for subjecting all comers to examination, and requiring ecclesiastical passports? The truth is, while Heaven's last and most fearful ban unquestionably rests on insincerity in every shape of worship or life, each one's sincerity, there being no evidence to the contrary, must on earth be taken for granted in what he does; and the common maxim of the law here, too, is in force, that innocence must be presumed until guilt is proved. Sincerity is a virtue whose claim and risk every one must especially put on himself; for who can pierce the human breast with instruments from the Church, or the Most High, to gauge degrees of truthfulness in different men! When, indeed, all defences and tests are gathered around the Lord's table, can no insincere persons reach it? With — nay, on account of —

such defences and tests, will no sincere persons, devoutly loving him as their Saviour, stay away?

Moreover, this grand objection lies against so emphasizing sincerity in an ecclesiastical rite, that it presents sincerity as a limitary and technical quality, and so leads to boundless corruption in the very sanctuary. All history shows that restricting the quality of virtue to any select points of outward circumstance depraves the human mind. What but this principle of a peculiar holiness in formal acts and ordinances of piety made the blackest transgressions in the Romish Church venial, if only the transgressors were ritually correct and pure! What but this led to that sale of actual indulgences for sin, which brought in the Reformation like a thunder-cloud in a foul and murky sky! What but this has been the apology for tortures and massacres without number or bound, and for even choosing some Bartholomew's day for the utmost enormity of cruelty and crime, a human sacrifice of Huguenot blood being thought, after the example of the most brutal and savage religions, a proper addition to the worship of the saint! What but the same wicked principle did Jesus condemn, when he rebuked those who neglected their parents on the pretence that the sum which might have been contributed to their support was Corban, a sacred offering!

For the sake of the Church itself, as well as the world, then, I say, it will not do to take any other ground than that of sincerity as an ever-imperative and universal bond. There is such a thing as sincerity in our homes, in society, friendship, business! Is it of more concern in the temple, and of less in these things? Then in these it may be excusable, and have some grain of justification in private relations and common life! No, the safety, as the truth which alone is ever safe, is in its being, not a circumstantial, but essential excellence, whose violation is heinous in all cases alike.

What matters it where a man lies, if he lies? Is a cheat in the temple no cheat out of it? or does it become insignificant in the shop or the street? Ah! has the superstition which would localize religion within the terms of a ritual, and the confines of altar and shrine, nothing to do with the huge disclosures of practical iniquity, the defalcations of pecuniary trust, and the profligacies of political action, by which our own community has been astounded, and millions of its members wronged? "The temple of God is holy, which temple ye are." Where, then, is the temple of God? Is it altogether within those four walls of wood and stone, beneath that lofty spire you have reared and builded, and given with peculiar consecration to Him? or does it stretch its dimensions through His universe, and make all iniquity of deceit a profanation and sacrilege? Where is the Lord's table? Nowhere but within the railing with which it has been girded round in your meeting-house, or by the narrowness of your sect? No, it is wherever his disciples sit with mutual love, and love to him, to eat together, though but a crust of bread, and to drink but the cup of cold water to the brotherly giving of which he affixes an emphatic reward. The Master's rebuke — which fell on the Pharisee's hypocrisy not as it was shown in the synagogue alone, but by the wayside and in the dwelling, through the whole tangle of their daily falseness — will visit our insincerity in every place and with every wound it gives to kinsfolk or fellow-creature, as well as when with it we crucify him afresh as we sit at his board. No particular act or manifestation, but the entire spirit and design of evil, is it his custom and the genius of his religion to denounce; for not at Mount Gerizim or Jerusalem, but everywhere, we hear his word sounding, — "Now they have no cloak for their sin."

When he forbids his followers to swear at all, either by heaven or earth or the holy city, on the ground that an oath can produce no effect, even so much as to make one hair white or black, and allows nothing but the simplicity of yea or nay in our communication, what does he imply but that no sacred references or names can enhance the pure worth of sincerity in its most familiar manifestations? Nay, by enumerating together, does he not with one morality equalize God's throne in heaven, footstool on earth, the city of the Great King, and a man's own head, as entering alike improperly into the terms of an oath? In the Epistles, too, while we are exhorted to observe the feast with the unleavened bread of sincerity and truth, no more stress is laid upon sincerity at the table than elsewhere; but we are charged to be "sincere and without offence unto the coming of the Lord" everywhere. Christ's injunction to worship the Father in spirit and in truth, and David's declaration that only he who has clean hands and a pure heart can ascend into the hill of the Lord and dwell in his holy place, put sincerity in every private or public act of homage to the Most High on the same footing with sincerity in the celebration of any visible sacrament so called. The whole Bible, withering with its old and everlasting reproof those who speak deceitfully for God, as much as those who commit perjury in a court on their own account, is the voice of reason and conscience too. "He will lie for his side and lie for liberty," it was lately said of an active character in the political world. But liberty is truth, and accepts no such suicidal sacrifices! When we are told to love one another with a pure heart, is the prescribed sincerity of that love of less moment than the sincere carrying to our lips of a morsel of bread and a drop of wine in the communion? When the Pharisees imputed the miraculous works of Jesus to Beelzebub, though they did not in their heart believe what with their mouth they said, and he, in the most remarkable of all his denunciations, affirms their insincerity to be an unpardonable sin, did he consider their guilt less than if an opportunity had been given them of showing the same disposition in partaking the memorials of his body and blood? No, — the dictate of reason, that sincerity is a divine and fundamental trait of the soul, and that the least limiting of it to a singular sense or special function takes out its heart and life, and makes it a merely conventional thing, is confirmed in the greatest variety of Scripture expressions.

As respects Jesus himself, whom we commemorate in the Supper, and whom surely it is a grievous offence for any to commemorate otherwise than sincerely, it may almost be said that his chosen and peculiar characteristic, among other teachers, is the weight he lays upon sincerity in every word and deed. This absolute morality is well esteemed a chief title of his religion to a duration no other system can usurp or supersede. Nothing he cannot forgive, but hypocrisy. Nothing he cannot bear or away with, but a double mind. Nothing moves him for a moment to be angry or impatient, but a person's meaning one thing and saying another. It makes no difference to him what the particular instance or connection of the fault is, in or out of doors, on the threshold of the house or at the gate of the synagogue, during holy time or a week-day. The insincerity itself to his mind unhallows all, desecrates every spot, and disowns the unmeasured presence of God. It is blasphemy against the Holy Ghost, which he considers infinitely worse than blasphemy against himself: for is not this the reason of the distinction taken in that famous passage, that his earthly life or person was finite, but the Holy Spirit infinite? Therefore he would esteem it no aggravation of that whose vileness cannot be aggravated, that it should be committed against his memory in the Supper, as it was committed against his living presence in the flesh. In whatsoever it may occur, treachery is his aversion. He marks nobody with fire but the hypocrite, and the score of his finger is equally deep upon false play in the court or field, by the pit whereinto the ox is fallen and in the recess of the Holy of Holies. His imperative demand is of an honest purpose, for which he will overlook all defects of forgetfulness of mind or infirmity of will. On the poor, exhausted victims of vicious appetite less deep than on the treacherous he presses the brand of reproach. He has always for the weak a word of mercy and tender encouragement, averring that the publicans and harlots go into the kingdom of Heaven before the self-righteous and deceitful Pharisees. Fraud is his insuperable abhorrence; and his hatred of it is such, that, in specifying many of its multiplied examples, he emphasizes none; so that we should be surprised to find how many of his warnings could be reduced to this single point, — as if he had through all his discourses and parables but one command, — or rather as though sincerity were in his esteem the innermost essence and soul of every virtue and exercise, — worship, love, charity, — all action, expression, speech to God or man.

To commemorate such a person as this, who was not so much true as the truth, and who ascribed to truth in its action on the minds of men every triumph of sanctifying as well as illuminating power, — to commemorate him in the way of mere pretension and dead formalism, is a baseness of treason which could have no more inappropriate display. But the treason is just as unacceptable to him in the privacy of our room, under the cover of darkness, in the mental solitude of our most secret aims, or the tie that should loyally bind us to a single companion in the world.

Let me add, this Christian doctrine of sincerity, as a trait of worth essential and universal, draws forth or extorts the approbation of the human soul. What stirs and kindles us is this, — that the sincere man will keep the gracious festival his Lord has permitted, as he does everything, sincerely. His sincerity is not an accident or a robe, but a quality, reaching from and to the core of his being. Whatsoever his motion or performance, his sincerity will run into it and through it, as the property of a growing plant does into every limb and blossom, spray or leaf; and as, in medicine or the arts, it is often indifferent whether the virtuous juice needed be an extract from bark or root, pith or flower, so the mouth and eye and very finger of a true man will be sincere, — as Shakespeare says, the very foot will speak! But the hypocrite will, in his business, domestic life, and ordinary behavior, be a solemn pretender, whose conduct is just as abhorrent in the eye of God when he smooths his face to deception in the market, or makes it mask his purpose in his talk with a neighbor, as when he takes the elements with no feeling or emulation of the self-sacrifice which to all ages they represent.

Surely I would share that repugnance to insincerity at the Lord's table, which is at the bottom of the objection whose validity I do not allow. It is an affront to come not caring for Jesus, insensible of his divine excellency, untouched by his supreme beauty, and unsympathetic with his surpassing loveliness. Our wonder and incredulity exclaim, Who and how many of such persons can care to come? Of one thing there can be no doubt. More will come thus falsely, according as we magnify the credit and glory of merely coming. But more or less as they may be, how shall they be excluded? By no sentinels or inquisitors in office from the old Inquisition down! Curious locks, tough doors, and iron cages have been contrived to secure the treasures of banks, the riches of museums, and the regalia of kings. But whosoever of subtle temper may incline to approach the table, fancying some reason of honor or gain, there is proof enough that no bolt can be devised by any ecclesiastical inventor effectually to keep him out. He must be left to his inevitable reckoning with God.

If, in fine, sincerely, and on conscientious grounds, any, like the whole body of the Quakers, should abstain wholly from administering or receiving the Lord's Supper, because they think God requires a purely spiritual service, and his Son did not mean the transformation he made of the Jewish Passover to be perpetuated after Judaism itself should cease, shall their abstinence be esteemed a fatal defect, and a coming short of salvation itself? Rome answers, Yes. Every Protestant who likewise answers it, is a Romanist in spirit, whatever he be in name; for to this conclusion, be it frankly said, our argument inevitably conducts, that the point of supreme obligation, bearing equally on every human creature, without exception, is not the Lord's Supper, as the object for which our sincerity may qualify us, but is sincerity itself as the object of a spiritual struggle, in which different persons may to different customs, and in various external directions, be led.

I know, it is sometimes said, to frighten dissenters, that sincerity is not enough without a correct faith and style of worship. If it is meant in this statement to include what God does to save us, as no less needful than what we do ourselves, it is undoubtedly true. Sincerity, truly, is not enough, because man, with all his powers and qualities, is not enough. But if, as it appears, it refer to our own doing simply, the statement is palpably false. Sincerity, on our part, is enough. Sincerity of thought, desire, and purpose must, on our part, be enough; for verily it is all we have to offer. It is not possible for us to give anything else, or anything more. It is our thought and heart and soul! It is the love of the truth; and the love of the truth is in the eye of God of more price than its possession, so often neglected or abused. Be sincere, in relation to this service, is all we can ask. I am willing, said a great preacher to his hearers, that you should follow your own real conviction, whithersoever it may lead. What criterion other than this does God's Providence, or Word, or Spirit set before our minds? It cannot fail to guide us in the path of duty, to communion with his Son and fellowship with himself.

CHAPTER X.

SACREDNESS.

It is objected to open communion, that to all it exposes those elements which are too sacred to be touched save by peculiarly prepared persons. But was this Christ's idea? What are the elements but memorials of him, illustrations to us of that living flesh and blood in which his wonderful soul was incarnate? Did he then consider himself, whom the elements but distantly shadow forth, too sacred to be approached or touched by ordinary people? Did he, like kings, so often with unintended irony called sacred and anointed, shut himself up from the crowd, and avoid the pressure of the vulgar, or even the bad? He, that would share a draught at Jacob's well with the woman of Samaria, and offered to give her the water extinguishing all thirst; he, that was thronged with the multitude, and ate with the despised, — *he* sequestrating the symbols of his presence from the people now! Was the bread he touched with his own hands, and passed round some table in Judæa, less sacred than that made ready by any mortal servant of his truth? With what beggar by the wayside would he not have shared his crust? Considering what his character was, do we honor or dishonor it by this fancied dignity of its outward seclusion from mankind? Verily, the more he is touched, the better!

This is the quality of a truly sacred thing, not that it must be handled with tender and fearful fingers, but that it can bear to be exposed. Its sacredness is too real and great to be wasted or lost. What can or must be superstitiously hid, is but of a weak and delicate purity. What, like the lady in Comus, is able to pass unhurt through all gloom and peril of the open world, is holy indeed. So, as with none beside, was it with our Lord. If the hem of his garment was not forbidden to the diseased woman whom Satan had smitten so long, shall the board human hands have fashioned for him, though it was never near him on earth, be fenced round against the access of any whom conceit of our own holiness counts profane? True, the table is sacred. But the sacredness of it, as of anything, consists not in its being set apart *from* any class of men, but set apart *for* a peculiar purpose, to be used for no other or inferior purpose under heaven. It is thus made sacred or consecrated, not by us as distinguished from other or worse men, but by the Lord himself, with his own love and sacrifice. Our ministry does not, like the Romish priesthood, pretend, by customary words solemnly pronounced over the elements, to consecrate them. We do not claim, as servants at the altar, to reserve the cup to ourselves as too sacred to be shared by the laity, of whom we hold the clergy as but a part, flesh of their flesh, and bone of their bone.

Taking, not vague feeling, but intelligent thought for our guide, we shall continue the discriminations thus well begun. If we ascribe to the elements either a sacredness on account of their belonging to a minority of human creatures to partake, or an intrinsic and substantial sacredness in their own form and composition, we rejoin the party of Rome in that superstitious addition to original Christianity, which, once allowed, will carry us on in the line of absurdity, we know not to what extreme and interminable length. That party regards the bread and wine as converted into the very body and blood of the Lord, no reality, but only the accidents and appearances of bread and wine being left; — which miracle, even could it be imagined so cheaply wrought at every unnumbered celebration in their Church of the Eucharist, would, to a rational soul, have no advantage to atone for its strangeness; inasmuch as it is not the body and blood, but only the spirit and life of the Lord, that we want, or that can do us any good. If Apostles could say, "Though we have known Christ after the flesh, yet henceforth know we him no more," surely we can crave no such fleshly manifestation as the Romish theory maintains. Beside the failure of this theory to answer any noble end in its direct application, it is only disgusting and offensive to the very imagination to follow the directions it requires as to the treatment of such morsels of the loaf as may have dropped, or not been consumed or passed through the course of nature, or been exposed to the agencies of decay. A decent writer will not burden the memory or hurt the delicacy of his readers by any attempt at their enumeration. In perusing some grave treatises of Romish authors, the physiology of animal processes, rather than exercises of experimental religion, seems to become the actual topic, to which, by false theories, the writers have been driven, but from whose gross or morbid treatment the mind shrinks in disgust.

In truth, not a party in the general Church, but the very reason and heart of humanity, protest against the doctrine of sacredness, which, in its technical mode, arbitrary extent, and the things it includes, Rome has made at once so childish to provoke ridicule and cruel to inflict pain. Curious inversions and self-contradictions in defining *the holy*, her history contains indeed! When some holy thinker, some saintly heretic, for bursting forms which he has outgrown, and soaring above dogmas he cannot endure, has been burned in the fire, or tortured to death on the rack, and then condemned to be buried in unconsecrated ground, we may well ask, pursuing the very line of our theme, What is it that can make a burial-place sacred? An ecclesiastical ceremony, with bell or book, performed by one even the wickedness of whose character, as the theory expressly requires, cannot take away the virtue of an office done in his sacramental order? Does this cause any soil to be a sacred enclosure, in the beautiful German title *God's acre*, and a fit place for the rest of his children? No, the holy man that lays down at last the load of his mortality, whom not flame nor axe—nothing—can touch further, himself hallows for ever before God and in human memory the spot of his repose; nor could robed processions, or hired choristers, or the tall plumes that, from temple-doors, the traveller sees darken the streets of foreign towns, or whatsoever final rites, add to the holiness which is the only true odor of sanctity from the soul. God's presence made the place holy where Moses was admonished to put off the shoes from his feet; and God's presence, in the sense of peculiar favor, must be over the very ashes of those who have done and accepted his will. When the French poet, Béranger, who knew neither ambition nor obsequiousness, and would not flatter the people or be servile to the court, is laid in his grave, though through the confusions of the Church he could rise to no clear and certain statement of his own faith, who of us, as if it could affect at all his futurity, cares for the ground he is borne to, with stealthy track and a military guard, lest the fall of a man should be the revolution of an empire?

Such illustrations, certainly, so far from eliminating the idea of sacredness, show it residing, not in the outward thing, but in the feeling of the heart. Not holy things, but holy persons, our religion mainly requires. "Be ye holy, for I am holy." But what numbers of people will insist on any amount of holiness without, but upon none within themselves! That is holy or sacred over which any fresh devotion or heroism has thrown its charm. When the mother sinks with her babe in the watery sepulchre no spade has dug, because without her child she chooses not to be saved herself, the act to all maternal affection throughout the world is sacred, — nay, sacred to all human feeling, let me rather say. When the hunted fugitive from bondage trusts herself with her offspring to the floating ice to cross the Ohio River, rather than fall, for what fate she knows not, into the hands of her pursuers, on such perilous footing not daring to follow, those cold blocks, melting under her feet and floating southward to the abandoned land of captivity, become as holy as any temple in old cities of refuge, or as the horns of any altar to which the wretched ever clung. We touch heaven, said one, when we lay our hand on a human body. Truly so we do, if that body be the tabernacle of a righteous soul; for heaven is not a fixed territory, with boundary lines like an earthly kingdom, but the habitation of the good, reside they where they may.

So far from disowning or restricting, would

we might extend the quality of sacredness to a thousand things now held profane! Would there might be a sacredness in week-days as well as Sundays, as there was in God's working no less than in his rest! How many still think the sacredness of the Sabbath must be observed by staying closely within doors during all the hours spared from the sanctuary,—as if a house built by man could be more holy than altars of rock, temples of hills, and forest cathedrals reared by God, or to sit in a chair more holy than to walk forth and meditate with the patriarch at eventide! Would there might be some sacredness in other books that we write, and that modern authors publish, as well as such overflowing sanctity in the ancient and Holy Bible! Let us not be partial to the oath, however earnest, that invokes the sacred heavens, — for the earth we tread should be sacred also. Human beings, familiar as they are with one another, should never be brought by familiarity into contempt, or let what they call their love be so light a thing it can degenerate into disrespect; but, in their common dealings, in their domestic and friendly ties, let them be sacred to one another! Let the Lord's Supper be sacred. Too sacred it cannot be. But shall every other supper that we eat be unholy, and every circle at the tables in our houses gather for the supply of animal wants alone? Or, in the noble sentiment of the Apostle, being "debtors to the flesh not to live after the flesh," shall bread of immortal life be mixed with outward nutriment on which our spirits feed, as our hands help, while a purged vision beholds the Lord of our redemption, always one of our number, as truly as when, after his resurrection, he entered the closed doors of the chamber, or ate with his disciples on the borders of the Galilean lake, or as in the Real Presence, which it is no monopoly of the Ultramontane Church, but the common privilege of Christians, to find in the feast? O how much, in matters how manifold, are we to hold sacred! Is it said, the elements have a sacredness all their own? Beware, lest exclusive consecrating them desecrate all beside! We cannot over-consecrate one thing, without unhallowing another. We cannot make an artificial virtue, without taking from the horror of a real vice; nor turn an innocent into a guilty act, without hurting all purity. If it be as bad to taste wine, or dance, or witness a dramatic representation, as to lie or steal, then to lie or steal is no worse than a temperate pleasure of the lips, or the feet, or the eyes. To be bitter, bigoted, exclusive, and censorious, some seem to consider a righteousness in themselves which cannot consort or have fellowship with any one who does not, contrary to Christ's prayer for his disciples, come "out of the world."

To make the bread and wine alone or distinctly sacred, is to profane that common life, every breath of which we draw from God, and all whose pulses come from the beating of the Father's bosom. What is specially sacred in the Supper is not a height and degree of sacredness to which nothing else can attain, but the particular, the ever lovely and venerable sacredness of those final circumstances in our Lord's career, from which its meaning comes. Does any one say, Such a sinner as I am, unjust, sensual, unprofitable, cannot take that hallowed bread and wine? But how much, precisely what amount of sin in our designs or our appetites do we find ourselves able to accommodate with the other exercises of religion,—with our regular worship, with the secret prostrations and vows of our closet, with the baptism of our children, with the providence of God in the chambers of our sick ones, with the funeral prayers spoken over our dead, and with the tombs we build to their memory, and should visit with a sorrow as sacred as the worship that ever newly dedicates the temples of Almighty God?

But be the things which should be considered sacred fewer or more, how illogical the conclusion that anything on account of its sacredness should be closed from human beings! Rather let it be opened to all. It is sacred, says the objector, and therefore should not be opened. It is sacred, I answer, and therefore should be opened. The sacredness of a thing is a reason always for its being opened; as the mystery of a thing, to the soul of inspiration, is a reason for its being revealed. God's house is sacred, and for that reason should be, not shut, but open to all. The Bible is sacred, and should not be kept from the people, as priests have kept it, but wide open. Only what is unholy should be closed and forbidden. The sacraments, all of them, because they are such, should be open, — the Supper among the rest. Is the rite Jesus instituted any more sacred than the words he spoke? If not, as they are to our reading, let it be open to our gaze and hands and lips! Let its sacredness, like as of some powerful aroma, be diffused among the abodes of men, through the roads of countries, the streets of cities, the shops of merchandise, and the halls of pleasure. Let it be a holy mountain air, purity from the sea, or the incorruptible sunshine with healing on its wings, so that what is already sacred may make sacred all beside!

In order to this, verily it only needs we should learn what sacredness is. What are sacred places, compared with the thoughts of holy pilgrims by whom they are visited? What are the bones and sacred relics of dead saints, compared with the sanctity that lives and works wonders of mercy before our eyes? What is any vast society or church, compared to the human soul? Well, by solitary waysides, do we salute, not our friends and acquaintances alone, but our humanity in the form of strangers; for no dead and senseless thing is so sacred as the living humanity that is God's child. Sacred is the feast, but more sacred the guest. Only when we understand this, will consecration become a fact in the world, as well as an idea and a name.

10

CHAPTER XI.

COMMONNESS.

It is objected to open communion, that it is making the Lord's Supper too common. This objection is urged from the quarter of those who do not partake of it, as well as that of communicants. It proceeds on the idea that there must be in religion something which is not laid bare to the common view; and is, in fact, only a re-statement, on another side, of the objection last considered, respecting the sacredness of the rite. This notion of something which a few may perceive and enjoy, but which must nowise be extended to the commonalty of the world, is a very old and prevalent objection, both in things civil and ecclesiastical. Somewhat dark and restricted, in apartments, proceedings, and ceremonies, has been connected especially with all religious systems. First came the heathen mysteries and the adyta of heathen temples, with solemnities often as impure as they were concealed, — examples indeed of the truth of Christ's words about the deeds of darkness. The reservation of the cup to the priesthood of Rome in the Eucharist is only one instance of carrying out but too faithfully, against the spirit of the Lord, the old secrecy; and the exclusiveness which admits but a favored few to the table can be regarded in no other light than as a continuation, however faint and slender, of the same.

I shall not enter into a discussion of the value or disservice to the world at large of mysteries in religion. I shall not undertake to say how far their evil has been counteracted by some use in rude ages and for uninstructed people; nor whether God himself may not have winked at the times of this ignorance. It concerns me here only to maintain that ordinances of mystery do not exist in the Gospel, but are departures from the whole spirit of Christianity, and that there is no hint, especially in regard to the Supper, of anything done privately as in a corner. The Author of our religion did not keep himself, in any of his sayings or doings, aloof from the multitude. He had his particular friends; he had his chosen disciples; but what he communicated to them he would communicate to all, in parables if they could not understand it spiritually; and he declared plainly, that whosoever did the will of God was dear to him as mother, sister, or brother. He was the most extraordinary being that has ever lived on earth; he was let down in hands of miracle from heaven; he was of his own kind, not man, or angel, or deity, yet fashioned as in a threefold cord of them all; yet, notwithstanding, he made himself the most common person that has ever lived. None so lowly or universal as he. His immense soul and mighty life stretched over the whole compass of humanity, and embraced all orders and conditions of men. The Jews would have kept him to themselves. He was crucified as a malefactor because he would not consent to be a temporal king. Those Hebrews who became Christian converts would have confined his doctrine to the small measure of their traditionary expectations, legal customs, or political plans; but they could not so cramp its nature. It was too broad and expansive. The oak they would have planted in an earthen jar shattered their frail code with their antiquated pride to atoms. There is nothing which Jesus practised or proposed, but has this unlimited character. Universality, commonness, is written all over his truths and laws and emblems; and, in the absence of the least intimation to any such effect, it is impossible to conceive that he intended his Supper for an exclusive privilege. Rather would he open it on every side, thus harmonizing and symbolizing, as he did always with the natural work and the ordinary providence of God.

All the best things which it pleases our Maker to bestow, he makes common to his creatures, — the air, the light, the ground under our feet, the heavens over our heads. The sea rolls it waves, shows its majesty, and offers its liquid floor, not to nobles and lords, but to all who would gaze upon or move over it. The stars wear no veils, and roll in no partial courses, but are wonderfully arranged to display their measureless grandeur to every most tender and feeble eye; nor is there a point on the earth which does not command the breadth of the skies. All great inventions, printing, the compass, steam, with its numberless relations and inexhaustible uses for locomotion and manufacture, every art that contributes to human comfort, the medicine that heals disease, the ether that lulls mortal agony to sleep, are for the common wealth and good. Shall the little cable, whose finger-sized cord we yet hope to stretch through the Atlantic depths, be for the glory of any class or any private pleasure or gain? No, its slender wires shall convey knowledge through the gloomy caves of the sea for the obscure and humble, as well as for crowned heads and presidents. For every student of events and for every lover of his race shall gracious news or solemn tidings flash from shore to shore, as well as for the statesman in his office, or the opulent merchant at his desk. Intelligence, on those mysterious wings of flame that can fly beneath the fathomless waves, shall come of the fortunes of friends travelling in distant parts, and the health of kindred dwelling far away, as well as of the price of goods, the rise and fall of stocks, or vast revolutions of the wheels of human policy. The lightnings shall be man's servants to announce birth and death, that so alter the world to individuals and families, as well as the flourishing and downfall of empires. With their subtile blaze along the slender threads of wire, as potent to purge the public mind as their discharges from the volumed rolling vapors are to purify the atmosphere, they shall scatter the clouds of misunderstanding between men and nations, sweeten the world's sentiment, and be the silent keepers of its peace. The benefit will be great, and therefore must be common, as, on God's system of the universe, all great benefits are.

But of nothing, in any material or economical department of human life, is it more true, than of the highest sphere of our religion. It was not for your, or my, but everybody's solace and salvation, that the angels sang, Glory to God in the highest, peace on earth, and good-will to men! It was not for citizen or countryman, for obscure or famous, unlettered or wise, white or black, good or bad alone, that the Saviour was born, but for every race and kindred and tribe and tongue. Nor was it for those who have agreed to certain dogmas, passed through prescribed processes, or been affected with conventional experiences of any theological sect, that Saviour spreads his table and gives his invitations. It was for whosoever will come. It was for every one hungry and athirst. It was for all whom the broken loaf, that was his body, can strengthen, or the flowing wine, that was his blood, can refresh.

The objection, therefore, to our doctrine, instead of implying its untruth or disadvantage, is, on the contrary, its very recommendation and seal. If it makes the table common, it makes it what it should be and was meant to be. The Apostle Peter was a just expositor of his Master's mind, when, being miraculously stirred to extend the new religion to the Gentiles, he justified himself against all narrow, Jewish rebuke by declaring, with the great, miraculous sheet for his voucher, God had taught him to esteem nothing common or unclean. What words more sublime and cheering to the human soul, to all of us, who are made of common clay, and endowed with common faculties, were ever uttered! I object, then, to the objection, that it goes on the discouraging and fatal assumption, that what is common must of course be low and bad, that the common sight must profane, and the common touch soil everything; an assumption how contradictory to our Lord's teaching, and may I not say to our Lord's experience! Not the reputable and distinguished persons furthered him, but the common people heard him gladly, and all the people rejoiced for all the glorious things that were done by him. Not the people of Judæa, but a faction of the Jewish church and state, persecuted and crucified him. Not his nation, but its proud and bigoted rulers, were his foes. Let us not admit the wretched and dispiriting doctrine, that what is common, or made common, must somehow be poor, vicious, unprincipled, and false; but believe it may of God be permitted to become pure and faithful, high in honor, and bright with the beauty of holiness.

The making the religion of Jesus, in all its parts, of form or teaching, common and universal, will tend, with a virtue that belongs to no other agency, to this certain result. Universality is the very soul and spirit of the age, caused to be so by that Gospel, which, first of all things on earth, had it for its spirit and soul. The more common that Gospel is, in its facts, instructions, and emblems, the better; for then the wider will be their sanctifying power. We ought, verily, as soon to think of the grass and flowers and fruits of the earth being too common, of our friendly salutations and domestic affections being too common, or of a public spirit in the ties of civil duty too diffused, as of any part of our religion being too common. For a thing to be common is not for it to be worthless, as is so hastily and miserably taken for granted, insulting all human nature and human life, rather for it to be supremely worthy. No word so sickens the heart to hear, as *common* in the sense of base and wrong. So far therefore, from wishing to seclude the table from public participation and regard, I am free to say, we cannot make its hospitality too wide.

Marvellous enlargement has there not already been, through all ages and climes, of that narrow and ill-furnished board where the Twelve with their Master reclined! Shall it not yet reach round the earth, and assemble to itself all mankind, as the disciples of a common Saviour, the children of a common Father, whose honor will be exalted as it is wide?

If it be asked, what then shall prevent the festival, that is so common, from being cheap, I answer, the spirit and force thrown into its administration. If no feeling is brought to the form by minister or people, none will pass through it or be carried away. It is no generator of holiness, but only a channel. It will express, and by expressing confirm, the devotion with which it is observed. But when coldness sits in the chair, the table will be unaffecting and cold. It is no medium for the working of miracles upon the unbelieving and dead. For He who denied his mighty works to such on earth will not perform them from heaven. Here, too, to him that hath shall be given. Not alone who shall partake, but who shall administer it, is a question.

But why should the publicity of this particular ordinance destroy its solemnity? The solemnity of no other service of religion depends on a scanty attendance. Public worship is more solemn in proportion to the numbers gathered with one consent, awed before the voice of truth or the accents of praise melted with pathos or still as flocks of winged creatures, that hold one flying shape through the sky, in the height of common ecstasy The solemnity of the Supper may well be put into something other than its exclusive observance, into the meaning and power too of its exercise, the earnest feeling of the approaching communicants, the revival by mutual sympathy of the tender associations of the original scene, which, for every one of the handful they first bound, have stretched their spell now over hundreds of millions.

But if it be said that, in this common participation, many present will not fully appreciate what is done, I reply, neither did the first participants, at the time of their participation. They did not understand their Master's principles; they faintly imagined his aims; they were not disabused of their notions of his temporal sway; they left him in the hour of trial, and broke their vows, though they expressed, doubtless, some sort of imperfect love for him in the feast. Christ did not make their full appreciation at the time the condition of the Supper they ate. Afterwards, when he had died and risen again, after they had witnessed dread facts without and felt gracious influences from the descending Holy Spirit within, they comprehended it more. Its very observance educated them, as it does us, to observe it. It opens more and more its own meaning, as we sit successive seasons at its table. Nobody understands it at the outset, as its repetition, with his own profounder meditations, will make him, and as he will when the deeper experiences of life, sickness, death, and sorrow, have been his mighty instructors.

Meantime, in this schooling of ignorant or half-informed pupils, who, I pray, is injured by making the Lord's Supper one of the les sons? Is any hurt done to the sacred servic itself? It is a picture, most simple, of fact most sublime in history. Do the crowds tha gaze at sacred pictures in the Vatican, or mas terpieces of imperishable beauty in the Louvre harm them with their eyes? Are the paint ings profaned, or are the persons profaned an accursed by beholding them? No, not mor than is the beauty of morning or evening, o the mountain, sunset, or sea, though the im mense splendor and inconceivable grace o these apparitions be half wasted on the mos of mankind. Nor can that spiritual beauty which is of finer touch and scope more vas than any expression of the face of nature, b spent or corrupted by any multitude it ma draw. Rather will the exclusiveness tha locks it up, as special wonders of nature b their legal owners are sometimes locked, ne tralize its import.

Physical forces, acting on material thing may be so combined as to exert on objects a once a forwarding and retarding power, whic we sometimes see causing a ball first for moment to move on, and then, untouched, turn and roll back. So by superstition is the Christian ordinance shorn of its virtue. No representations have so pierced the heart of savage or civilized man, as those of the closing passages of the life of Jesus. "Obey your marching orders!" with curt and quaint solemnity, said the Duke of Wellington to the young clergyman who doubted the expediency of sending forth missionaries into every far-off heathen land. Why should not "every creature," to whom the supreme order requires the Gospel to be preached, be admitted to view its rites? They make part of our grand system of social religion. What forms shall best promote social piety, or being religious together? Evidently and undeniably, those which all can and do share. Therefore the exclusiveness of the Supper hinders social religion, and a form, with strange self-contradiction, is made to prevent or limit the accomplishment of the end of all forms.

Moreover, history shows that there is no extent of absurdity and wrong to which this exclusive spirit, once admitted, will not lead.

In the end of the third and the beginning of the fourth centuries the Lord's Prayer was considered too holy to be uttered by unbaptized lips; for, it was said, none but the baptized could properly address the Almighty as their Father. We should not know whether at such an assumption to smile or be shocked. Surely we should pay no respect to it, but disown it even at the cost of our lives. The time will come — let us do something to hasten and anticipate it — when the reservation of the Lord's table will appear in the same light. Already no slight shadow is thrown on its administration by the indisposition of many liberal and noble minds to remain and partake of it, even if allowed, at a sectarian request. They feel it ceases thus to be the Lord's Supper, and becomes the supper of a few men. A distinguished and universally respected jurist, in the frequent journeyings which his official duty required, being not seldom where the communion was observed, we are told, on this very ground never stayed unless it was in distinct terms the Lord's Supper to which he was invited. There is

indeed a potent reason for open communion to be found in the sort and character of persons whom close communion excludes.

If, in fine, it be inquired where, on the ground of open communion, is the Church to be found at all, and what are its metes, bounds, and visible proportions, — I ask, will it argue its non-existence or ruin its character if it should appear truly immeasurable, and stretch far beyond the reach of our calculation or sight? Indeed, have its dimensions ever been taken since the Infinite Spirit of God, incarnate in the shape of his Son, made Humanity his abode? Who has walked about our Zion, marked her bulwarks, and considered her palaces, so that, like a scientific surveyor, he can render in his report to the generations of men? What sort of Church was it Jesus spoke of, against which the gates of hell should not prevail? One like an army in the field, or a tower on a hill? No, but a spiritual Church, universal in heaven as well as unlimited on earth, whose ranks were never counted, even as, in the Apocalypse of the celestial host, we are told no man could number them.

When I think of it, no little company or denomination, like the population of a city or the troops of a commander, comes into my mind; but only such as that grander language of the Apostle, — "the general assembly and church of the first-born"! When we can measure the Lord himself, we can measure the mansion in which he dwells. But sooner shall we compass the walls of that New Jerusalem, which the seer of the Revelation, with such gorgeous dimness of glory, paints. No Council of Nice or Trent, no party of Calvin or Luther, no Eastern or Western Synod, Establishment or Presbytery, no band of men ever in the world leagued together, and calling itself the Church, could describe or compose it. It is the honor of the Church, not its disgrace or defect, that no time tells its age, no space includes its magnitude, no figures can sum up its adherents. Moving in it while it moves in its march, as a foot-soldier does in an immense expedition, I am not curious to see its beginning or end. Coming still, still proceeding, as the eye turns back or forth, part already across the flood and part crossing, it has no bound.

Its visibleness is not its wholeness, but only a sign and token thereof; as are the face and expression, of the soul of a man.

To all this some may say, your reasoning is superfluous argument and lost labor, because, practically, the communion is open now. I answer, this is by no means fact, but only tendency, slowly becoming fact in some places. It is to strengthen this tendency, and increase the fact even by a little, that I speak. But, alas! there is no sign that any of us will see open communion universal in our day. Too strong is the influence of remaining bigotry, and the hereditary prejudice of a narrow faith. Too deep, must I not say, in some places at least, has been sunk that line of formal distinction, which is made, not of iron or steel, but of those potent words, *I am holier than thou.* Too long has the attempt been going on to remove God's upper and final judgment-seat, for a human court, to this lower earth. Too inveterate is the habit of weaving into a lash and sting, those circumstances in the life of Christ from which he meant should be extracted, for the already bleeding wounds of humanity, only an ointment and healing balm. But the time will come, let it come now with us, when no select portion alone shall be received to taste the Supper; but we shall go out into the highways and hedges, and, as Jesus orders, by his love compel them to come in!

But, supposing the approach to the communion made perfectly open and free, and the line of distinction between Church and Congregation taken up, there is still an objection, which, operating when severe terms attend the administration of the Supper, is untouched and unanswered though all restrictions were removed. Not a few have always declined every invitation to the table, however kind or expostulatory, on the ground of their unwillingness to assume the new obligations resting, as they conceive, on all who expressly commemorate the Lord. They fear they might not be faithful to their vows, and therefore they will not utter or seal them. Their logic is a short syllogism. If they make no profession, no profession can they disgrace. Remaining as they are, they are safe from the

Master's reproach, like one in the civil state, or army, who, undertaking no special commission, cannot be blamed or cashiered for treachery or neglect. A more baseless objection could not be proposed. We talk of the slippery foundation on which the wicked are supposed to stand, and where their feet will slide in due time. But this is no foundation at all. For what idea of the obligations lying on the human soul from its Inspirer and Judge, can he have, who imagines them increased or diminished in number, lightened or aggravated in weight, by any ritual act? What obligations are those which the non-communicant does not assume? The obligations of truth, justice, mercy, love to God or his fellow-creatures? Living in a Christian land, attending on Christian worship, acquainted from childhood with the Christian revelation, is he not bound, or anywise less bound, to love, obey, and imitate Jesus Christ, simply because he does not celebrate this feast at his board? The notion, as one on which practically to proceed, would be monstrous. Fairly to state is to refute it. Our spiritual obligations are not like the hamper a dumb creature of burden bears on his back, which can be put on or off; but they are ties running through the centre, and woven as fibres in the very constitution of the soul.

How and by what process can the eating of the bread, and drinking of the wine, be the acts solemn as they may, affect these ties? I know the Church itself is greatly responsible for the existence and prevalence of the objection I am considering. The ecclesiastical custom has been to impress with great emphasis upon new converts the fresh duties of their position, and to demand or imply their promise to discharge them. It is true, that they to whom God and Christ are for the first time made known, or who become peculiarly aware of a Divine relationship, become also *sensible* of obligations which, however real, had been latent, and, not appearing to their minds, could not be discharged in their lives. But in regard to us, who are all the children of the Church, and the late posterity of a pious ancestry, the first date of whose Christian belief is beyond our own reckoning in the backward vista of time, no such premises of even imagined deficient obligation can be maintained. The character and being of God, the teachings and spirit of Christ, — to whom among us are they best known, — to those within or without the pale of the nominal Church? Where shall we find the truest offspring of that old religious parentage? Who shall say whether among names the minister has recorded, or those possibly not even breathed in his ear? Does there exist on earth any church-record copy, to which we can refer, of the Lamb's book of life in heaven? Are even baptism and the Supper the sure certificates of entry on the roll he holds in his hand? She that sits on the seven hills may say so. But she has no response to her words save from a few political despots, yet occupying thrones that have rocked already, shaken by the imprisoned spirit of civil and religious liberty, and doomed to rock again, and more fearfully. We give no such echo. Alas! daily proofs of untrustworthy communicants forbid. We cannot tell, or make any outward sign a pledge of the fact, whose obligations are greatest, or whose are least, or what shades of difference may arise from diversities of knowledge, temptation, and opportunity we have no means accurately to measure or detect. Promises to meet our obligations cannot alter the obligations themselves, however broken promises may be additional sins. Shall I take my new harvest to pay my old debts? asked a great farmer of the West, not dissolving, however, but only disallowing, his obligations.

In general, with estimates and concessions God alone is competent to define, obligation for us all is the same; only the performance in individuals different. Yet is there an obstinate prepossession to the contrary, as unreasonable as it is hard to root out. We are told continually by those whom we would regard as candidates for Christians, or by their friends, that they are reluctant to take this particular step of partaking the Supper, because it seems to them inconsistent with some pursuits they would still follow, or some pleasures of the world in which they desire to indulge. But what enjoyment or occupation does or can this step make guilty, which was innocent before? and what, that is innocent and moderate, does it forbid? Rather, should I not ask, what act or gratification is right even for a worldling because he is a worldling, but wrong for the member of a religious body? Does the absentee from a meeting-house, or from any service solemnized therein, absent himself from the presence, the eye, or any of the laws, of his Maker? Can he get away even from that temple of His, which "is all space," and that "altar which is earth, sea, skies"? Though he offer no homage in that temple, and lay no sacrifice on that altar, ought he not? and, because he does not, is any evil conduct of his more excusable on that account, or only another sin against the Creator already offended by his forgetfulness and disregard? I trow God does not bind his statutes so loosely on his children's minds, or make them at all matters of accident and circumstance, appendages of a form which human will is free to practise or omit. No demoralization could be greater, wider, or more sure than that resulting from such easy license. Until it can be shown what part of the moral code is relaxed, or which of the ten commandments has been annulled, in favor of the lovers of themselves and of their own delights more than of God, or that even the new commandments Christ brought for his disciciples is less imperative for the most silent man in an assembly than for the loudest professor, the objection must be adjudged invalid altogether.

But it may be asked, Does not the communicant consecrate himself? I rejoin with asking, Is the non-communicant exempt from the duty of self-consecration? The old Pagan philosopher had sense to know that there was not one divine law for Athens and another for Rome, but the same sublime precept of justice was sempiternal for all men. So there is no one commandment for the religious votary and another for the devotee of business, or fashion, or pleasure. In one chain are bound the seeker after God and the seeker of himself. Men in their shops and halls, on the street and the wharf, think they are in a different sphere, and to be judged by different rules from those frequenting closets of meditation and places of prayer. But they will find that they belong alike to one system, just as comets belong to the same system with planets, empty as they may be in their own composition, and far into barrenness and gloom as they may rush from the enlivening beams of the common sun. Those most distant from each other God can reach with the same benediction upon fidelity or whip of retribution, as he brings back the wanderers of the sky. As to the difference between one and another, which is made by a profession of religion, little indeed is the sum — important as a profession may be — to which, standing alone, it amounts.

There is a profession by which one distinguishes himself from his fellow-creatures as better than the rest, upon the worthless and offensive peculiarity of which I have already remarked. But truly we are professors all together. We belong to Christendom by inheritance and a complete entering into possession of our estate. We are Christians by birth and nurture. The first disciples were minors, just beginning in the grace of God. But, by all rules, we in this age are past our Christian minority. All wrong-doing, by us or our children, is violation of the compact in which we are held. A house of worship is a profession of faith and spiritual renovation; — for what but actual hypocrisy is the outward structure itself, or its renovation, if our principles be unbuilt and our souls unregenerate? All our exercises in such a house are professions. Our children, soon as intelligence begins, are so many little professors of religion. This is but the supposition which our whole condition involves, that we are Christians, young and old. All our preaching proceeds and should proceed upon it, rebuking sin and short-coming as degeneracy and declension, to be contemplated with astonishment, not with equanimity, as in the regular course of things, and as proper thorns on natural thorn-trees. The doctrine of total depravity in a Christian community, by asserting and taking for granted the necessity of evil, legitimates all wrong; for what is inevitable is right. Vipers are not sinners. Human vipers, if such exist, are persons too bad and depraved for conscious guilt; and something of such a character John the Baptist and Jesus may have had in mind in using for particular classes such a term. Our hypothesis in regard to transgression should be its recreancy, not as the act of a heathen scarce knowing better, but the disloyalty of one who has tasted the heavenly things which he now falsely rejects. The theory of conversion, as universally needful instead of education in a Christian Church, is a confession that Christianity, working for so many ages, has not produced its effect on the generations of men, but has only touched individuals here and there,—a lesson, after near nineteen centuries of effort, almost of despair as to the final result.

But we believe, imperfect as the attainment is, the theory does injustice to the thing. Our religion has become as truly hereditary as ever was Adam's sin, or that of any of his descendants. He that commits sin among us does not perform a natural and necessary thing; he violates the law of the family to which he belongs, whose privileges he enjoys, and whose atmosphere he breathes. The necessity of sinning! This proposition has been thrown against the Perfectionists. But it is a strange sentence in a Christian land with which to rebuke believers in the dignity and perfectibility of human nature! It is a reproach to the Divine nature no less than to the human. We are of the family of God by a double claim of birth and adoption. The transgressor in a Christian community is not a child of Satan acting as he must, but a voluntary prodigal and traitor, breaking the laws of the body to which, as a member, he is bound. What would be thought of converting a child, that had grown up in the bosom of home, to the love of his father and mother, or to respect for their commands? As strange, alien, and needless ought religious conversion to be in a Christian flock. When Jesus said, "Feed my lambs," he showed this to be his mind; for of lambs what is predicable if innocency be not?

The idea and prompting of a Christian life are widely enough diffused among all classes in our congregations of worship to justify at least this ground of a general and uniform equality of obligation for all. No line of Scripture, no dictate of reason, can be quoted in proof of its variation on account of any external observance or act, omitted or done. No, the celebration of the Lord's Supper is not an imposing of new obligations, but an aid to the fulfilment of old, uncancelled ones; and those who punctually use that celebration employ a means helping them to render all the offices and dispositions which others as much as themselves owe to God and man. As respects obligations, indeed, we are all insolvent. How many ancient debts we have never paid! What a mass and heap of duties we have just begun to touch, in our attention to them altogether behind time! Shall we not avail ourselves of every assistance, such as this tender memorial affords, to advance us on our way?

A keen observer of nature has said, there is in the world a great deal of *unsatisfied law*,— that is, of tendency to results in those arts of life so beneficent to the human race, which is hindered by the mixture of other tendencies and prevented by the operation of lower laws.

This conflict of law in nature has its parallel in the soul. Whatever can disembarrass and give free course to the higher law in us, setting the soul forward in a course of improvement like that pursued by Nature through her cycles and æons, from the meanest order of vegetable and animal life, shall we not welcome as the grace of God? Such, indeed, is the ordinance of which I speak. It does not aggravate the burden. Diametrically opposite is its effect. It helps us on with the burden we bear.

What a difference in effect from making the communion no longer a misnomer, but indeed common! A new sense of responsibility will pervade the Church; parental duty in religion will be more moved for an explanation of this Christian office to the young; and all the members of a religious body, it may be hoped, will feel that something depends on them, as well as on the minister, for the planting and nurture of the holiest sentiments of our faith. We shall not, for we cannot, in this alteration, any of us, be the same as before. Every change of method, on any vital point, in proportion to its importance is attended with a spiritual change. For every fresh means of improvement which we sincerely use, we are the better. A new seeing and hearing of sacred things, by us and our children, will generate new thought and emotion, flowing from the older to the younger, without end, age after age. So let the Supper, like everything truly great, prove its virtue on a broad scale!

CHAPTER XII.

VEIL.

I FIND a significance for our subject in the record of the fact that, at the crucifixion of Jesus, "the veil of the temple was rent in twain, from the top to the bottom." If we ask why the veil of the temple was rent in twain, Scripture does not state, or commentators, so far as I have seen, conjecture; they leave it as a mere incident in the narrative, an unmeaning portent of the history. But, truly, in this world God made, of universal cause and effect, there must have been some reason why the veil was rent, as it would seem necessarily by a miracle directed like a sword, inasmuch as an earthquake could overturn towers and shake pyramids easier than part a thread. We read in the story that Richard's axe could not vie with Saladin's scimetar. A special Divine stroke must have been aimed in this case. Had the veil been rent by human agency, the question why would have been asked very soon, and the profaner of the temple hurried to answer at the Sanhedrim, if not first stoned to death by a Jewish mob; for, to the Hebrew imagination, this veil was the cover of what was most venerable in the institutions of Moses and most sacred in the worship of God. Made of blue and purple and scarlet and fine-twined linen, wrought with figured cherubim to the utmost perfection of ancient art, hung on pillars of precious wood, overlaid with gold, made fast by golden hooks in silver sockets, woven, as the Talmudical writers say, of seventy-two threads of wool, each thread having twenty-four strands, to a thickness of the breadth of the palm of a man's hand, solemnly washed by three hundred priests, and stretched to guard the ark of testimony and mercy-seat with its cloud of incense in that cubic apartment called the Holy of Holies,—dividing the Holy from the Most Holy, the great tapestry of the world,—of a texture so firm it is said no human strength, and no tempest or convulsion even, only a special prodigy for that very purpose, could have torn it,—the object of greatest awe and mystery on which the eyes of the people could rest,—there must have been some design or lesson or reason why, when at the crucifixion it was rent in twain from the top to the bottom. Why, comes the question back, was it cut so thoroughly, as if to put it beyond all repair?

Truly, not in words did the Divine purpose need to be told, so plain the effect to abolish that peculiar sanctity of place, appointed for a childish age as it was abused with an inveterate superstition, and to do away with that material distinction of Holy and Most Holy, by letting daylight of heaven into that dark, windowless recess, which only the high-priest once a year, with a bloody offering for sin, could visit. Not in vain, then, did the last breath of the expiring Jesus, on its way to heaven, blow this veil asunder; but to signify for ever, to all behind, Jew or Greek, that holiness is no matter of outward space, but of the living spirit. He only thus repeated in death the frequent teaching of his life, in his walk through corn-fields, preaching in fishing-boats, telling the Samaritan woman that not Jerusalem or Gerizim, but spirit and truth, was the illimitable region of God's praise; that leading an ox to water, pulling an ass or sheep out of a pit, comforting or healing a fellow-creature, as much as any form of prayer, was a Sabbath-day duty; and, in fine, that not when or where, but what, a man thinks and feels and does, is the holy or unholy thing.

Ah! how well, at the very moment the veil was marvellously rent, did he illustrate his own doctrine! What was the rending but the sudden passing out of all special holiness from that old withdrawing-room of Aaron and his successors to the open hill Calvary? How was that hallowed by the unparalleled purity which taught that only a divine temper can hallow any material spot, and which meant not to desecrate any point or recess, particularly of the temple, but to consecrate the earth and human life!

But is this a lesson we need? Is there any veil of our temple to be rent in twain? I can only, for answer, ask, Is there not? I know the sublime doxology we sing, —

> "To Thee, whose temple is all space,
> Whose altar earth, sea, skies," —

but to make or own such temple and altar, alas! how we forget! Every-day illustrations show it. Would the senators, that are wont to lay on each other such opprobrious epithets, and it may be vulgar, bloody blows, in their chamber, do it in the sanctuary? and, if not, do they remember the veil of artificial distinction of one place from another is torn away, and their chamber is a sanctuary of law and religion before God? Would the counsellors, that sometimes disgrace the court by adding to their client's litigation a quarrel with no nicety of terms among themselves, dishonor a house of prayer with the coarse or angry expressions they use? If not, do they bear in mind the rent veil at Jerusalem, and that the seat of justice also is a temple of God? Would the traders, that deceive in a bargain, or falsify a contract, as quietly offer a false profession of that religious feeling every one of us by entering these portals does profess, or an empty, senseless vow in divine songs and supplications? Then do they think that the shop, market, exchange, is part of the Most High's dwelling, that the veil between holy and most holy places has dropped at the word of God,— there is no outer and inner court? that, though we talk of the temple of Mammon, Mammon has no temple,— Christ having annexed the whole territory as divine? that every word they speak is serious as an oath in the heavenly ear, all lying is perjury,— no real distinction made by holding up a right hand, kissing a book, and kneeling at a shrine? and that Jesus drove the sellers of doves out of the ancient shrine, not merely because they were merchants there, but thieves, overreaching those with whom they dealt? Did the good man, of our own commercial circle, who pasted sacred sentences into his pocket-book, so that he might not fail to read them whenever he handled his money, put them, think you, into an unfit and unholy place of sacrilege? Nay, suspended in vestries in what votive tablets, carved for ecclesiastical ornaments by what sculptor's chisel, shining in splendor from the page of what illuminated Bible, are they more appropriate than on the purse of the wealthy, over the desk of the counting-room, or, far off along the world of waters, inside the vessel's forecastle, or on the quarter-deck?

Could you, my reader, let forth the ill-natured expression in tone or look at the communion-table of your Lord, which may possibly, without self-reproach, appear to wife, husband, parent (O God, forgive that!), to child, brother and sister, at your own daily board? Then has it not escaped your consideration that, by the token of that falling veil, your household-feast should be a sacrament of love and purity to the Omnipresent, whose Son ate with as much heavenly goodness in the abodes of men as in the upper room where he turned the Passover into his own Supper? The repentant Judas flung down the thirty pieces of silver, as we read, in the temple, as though in that dedicated place the sacrifice of his remorse might be more acceptable; but ah! he forgot no less it was in the universal temple, and under the immediate watch of

God, that he also stood, in that dark conclave of chief priests and captains, where he promised to betray his Master!

When we limit and localize our sanctities, we forget it is not only of holy times or holy places that Holy Writ speaks, but of holy hands and unadulterous eyes, a pure heart and feet in righteous ways, wherever hands or feet, heart or eyes, may look and beat and work and move. "The temple of God is holy, which temple ye are!" adds the Apostle, knowing, as he so well did, that, if holy places could save the world, there would be no danger of perdition, — enough of them could be contrived, — but that there must be also holy persons, affections, and deeds! I have seen temples and cathedrals in famous cities, jewels on the front of the globe, gleaming with polished marble, adorned with thousands of marble statues on a single one. But, without travelling, I have seen men and women, my brothers, my sisters, more truly temples to me; — their look purity, their countenance worship, in their eye aspiration beyond the tallest spire of the globe, whose height is boasted in the descriptions of him that has ascended to greet the sun; their simplest speech of God, not canting discord as speech of God sometimes is, but better music than in the organ-loft of St. Paul's or of the Madeleine, though the stop called the human voice were sounding. Yea, living and moving temples I have seen, more holy than were ever consecrated in wood and stone. The veil of the temple was rent, as its exclusive sanctity fled, that the human body and soul might become God's temple. I have seen a floating Bethel resounding with prayer and anthem, as it was moored now to one wharf in a great metropolis, and then made to swim to another; and I have heard hallelujahs from the cabin of the wave-tost ship pierce the calm heavens through the gusty winds. But when mortal flesh and blood quiver with grateful acknowledgments of almighty law and providential care, not bells or spoken orders, but the spirit within giving the signals so well obeyed through all the round of daily duty and blessing, and along the whole perhaps seventy years' path of life, — that is a moving temple, before which Solomon's dims its glistening plates, and Cologne stops unbuilt, and St. Peter's lowers its mighty dome!

"Know ye not that your body is the temple of the Holy Ghost which is in you?" When that body appears in its glory in the service of God, every lust extinguished before incorruptibly burning and all-purifying love, each worldly passion confessing and guided by the devoted will, like crouching lions at their keepers' feet, — lowly adoration touching the lips with a light as though Stephen looked up again with open vision, or St. Cecilia left the canvas or came down from the sky to sing once more on earth, — I think hymn-book, Bible, venerable building, and Sunday hour less precious in the Great Sight than the sanctified vitality which comprehends them all in the human soul!

Holiness a quality of punctual moments and measured ground? But, I ask you, will those moments and that ground, when reckoned only or particularly holy, suffice? By whom, then, have the profligacies and dishonesties you mourn over in these days still of defalcation and pollution, been done? Always by men that never saw church-spire, never lifted their eye to belfry at the street corner, never entered solemn precincts, and never sat at the table of the Lord? Would God, No, indignantly we might reply! But wherefore, and on the ground of what experience, do not a few begin to declare they feel less inclined to trust a man who professes a great deal? Wherefore, but because the name of so many a professing Christian, laying great stress on ordinances, coming out from the world, standing on the Lord's side, and belonging, like Saul *before* his conversion, to "the most straitest sect of our religion," for *he* never talked of belonging to it afterwards, — so many such a name is on the defaulting or sensual list, till people, with sarcastic reference, elsewhere than in the congregation sing, —

> "Can rites and forms and flaming zeal
> The breaches of thy precepts heal?"

The veiled woman of the East is no purer than the unveiled one of the West, if she be as pure; "the veiled prophet" is no more spotless than the open-browed one, to say the least; and the holiness that is loud on the tongue, but gives out in the conduct, sinks with lower depreciation than any bank or firm or bubble stock in the market! But if all this be so, what is the use of sacred exercises or enclosures at all? Of no use but a perverted one, if made to shut up imagined holiness like the veil Christ tore in the Jewish temple; but they are of use transcendent, if turned with power to cleanse all our behavior. Let the temple prove itself not useless or unholy, by overflowing into the world with odor of sanctity, as a flower keeps not its fragance in its cup, but fills with aroma the air! Let Sunday, like a declaration of peace lasting beyond the date of its signature, speak a truce to the strife of avarice and hate through the week, and there will be use! What is the use of a great magazine yonder? To keep things on the shelves, or to scatter utensils of comfort through a thousand homes? Of a manufactory the use? To pile up its goods, or to clothe and furnish the million? Of a telegraph the use? Merely to dot signs of letters, or control all business with its information? Of the reservoir the use? To contain water, or carry it to your third story? And of that round brick building on the city's edge the use? To generate an invisible gas, or to illuminate at nightfall the city?

So the use of a church does not end with the visible church, with our ceremonial, nay, or our emotion. To think so, to emphasize external modes, especially to make any mode a dividing line to sever the assembly in two, is to do what but patch up again the veil Christ rent, and substitute for spiritual regeneration ecclesiastical etiquette. Let us attend on religious services, if God give them grace to touch our soul, to elevate our avocation, and to sweeten our life. Let us come to them from the perhaps deteriorating course of our habits and affairs. They may, for use, serve at least like those metres of glass and metal which gauge degrees of light or atmospheric temperature and weight; and, our conscience being index, tell us how much purity, warmth, sunshine of elemental goodness, illustrate our career, — what weather is coming, glorious or lowering, with the days in our moral sky, —

and in our short-comings admonish us, with help of God and Christ, how we must increase the holy element to make our social climate unlike the atmosphere of some unhappy souls, one our fellow-creatures can live in here below, and like that

> "Where everlasting spring abides
> And never-withering flowers."

At the death of Cromwell and of Napoleon tempests vexed the air and tore the beautiful trees of the garden in pieces; fit close to their stormy, battling lives! When Jesus expired, while the sky was darkened, the earth quaked, the rocks were rent, the graves opened, and many bodies of saints arose, nothing was destroyed but a hurtful distinction; nothing was destroyed save that which kept men apart and alienated them from each other. Not the temple was overthrown; only the veil of the temple, which had been anticipated in some of the old Pagan recesses, was rent in twain. Let our temple stand, and we only pray God that the risen Lord of life may remove every barrier in it betwixt our souls! Let no distinction in its parts or services between holy and most holy, divine worship and special communion, such as existed in the Jewish fane and continues in many a Christian shrine, remain with us! — for that is the veil of our temple, precisely corresponding to the old one, which he, our Master, would rend in twain.

CHAPTER XIII.

MEANS.

Any one with the common modern notions of ordinances truly must be amazed that Paul did not, on account even of the Corinthian abuses of the Lord's Supper in selfish luxury and intoxication, forbid any to partake it; but, on the contrary, requires all the members of the assembly, instead of going separately, as some of the richer and more prosperous had been wont when they had finished their own feast, to tarry for one another, and partake all together. But, in the light of true Christianity and the Master's own mind, this will be no amazement at all. A special argument for open communion of the Lord's Supper to all is indeed contained in the fact, thus so boldly demonstrated, that the Supper is a means, not an end. If it were an end, a consummation of Christian excellence, then, of course, only those who have attained, and are already perfect, needing but that last step, would be admissible to it. The only ground on which its partial and exclusive character is anywhere sustained, is its being a stamp of the regenerate and redeemed, a finishing stroke, like the last touch on a painting or statue, of the grace of God. Now here the decisive question is, whether Jesus Christ himself so regarded or presented it.

The only answer possible to this question is that he did not. He expressly states it as a means, and a means alone. He never speaks of it otherwise. "Do this in remembrance of me," is his direction; that is, as a means of calling him to mind, and experiencing all the tender and holy influences which such a recollection of him, who was the very ideal of love and virtue, is suited to produce. Can we conceive of him desiring to be remembered as a matter of personal gratification, still more of making the remembrance itself, without reference to its beneficial effect, the object in view? No, he never dreamed of it as the stamp of accomplished virtue or spiritual termination of the pilgrims' path; but rather placed it at the beginning of their discipleship, an aid to their poor, imperfect understanding of his religion, instituted simply in order that they might comprehend it better and be guided by it more. So much for the question of authority. But moreover, let me add, from the very nature of the case, the Supper, as an outward act and ceremony, like all others that are outward, can and must be a means, and that only. The end of man, of his immortal soul, is not external, never in anything he can see or touch, taste or handle. The end is an invisible beauty and infinite sanctity, a boundless goodness and love. Principles, not formal practices, are ends; and principles can never be fully embodied in forms, or stated in words, but only perceived by the soul and pursued in the life.

The point being then established, that the Supper is a means, the next inquiry is, Who shall use it? Only the good and holy, only those who have made great progress in virtue, only those who are technically or truly described as having experienced religion? It will be difficult to say so, when we consider that a means is something to help one on, like extending a hand, affording nourishment, giving a direction, or in the darkness holding up a lamp to the traveller, who has indeed set out on his journey, but requires assistance to proceed further, and the particular time and place for whose encouragement should be determined, not by his speed or forwardness, which would dispense with and put aside all aids as only an encumbrance, but by his weakness, ignorance, and necessity. Accordingly, the Supper was once called *Viaticum*, refreshment by the road, such as a wayfarer might carry in his wallet or basket to strengthen him to continue in his course. To whom, then, should it be given, but to the faint, weary, and way-worn? — more at least to them than to the giants who have strode over obstacles, and actually won the race. Therefore, with good reason, not for a developed, spiritual manhood, but for those of doubtful and unassured moral ability to keep them from falling, and stimulate them in the better career, the Supper was by Jesus himself appointed. He never ceases to tell us his business is with the feeble and straying, the lost and sinful and sick. It was to draw them by the cords of sacred association, when things unseen and eternal could not attract them by their essential power and intrinsic charm. It was to make memory the friend of virtue, and past society a spur to lonely fidelity, and a spiritual presence more real to them by the signal of material circumstance.

The Supper ordained for the good or holy alone! Verily, they need it not! If they had been contemplated, if only the clean believer, righteous doer, and accomplished saint had been in Christ's mind as he went out of the world, such a rite as the Supper would not have been ordained at all. When the end is attained, means are employed no longer by God, or a wise man, or Jesus Christ, the Mediator from heaven. Had he been thinking only of those already by moral agencies made perfect, he would have let the Jewish Passover, temple and altar and priestly robe, and all, drop to the ground without such adoption, continuation, and interpretation into a nobler and more spiritual sense. To altogether worthy followers and bosom friends such a substitute for the Jewish ordinance would have been quite superfluous. They would have remembered Jesus truly, without any prescription or form of reminder. They would have held sufficing and glorious fellowship with him in their own souls. To them tables and vessels, bread and wine, would have been needless substances, if not baser elements.

No, not for such strong ones — but for imperfect, erring, and sinful men, in whom yet some feeling of love and admiration for the Great Deliverer had been awakened, who would emulate and every way reach up to his transcendent character — the table was spread, the loaf broken, and the cup poured. If it be said, this would exclude advanced Christians from the table, while admitting humble beginners, I reply, compared with that wondrous pattern God in his Son has let down from the heavens, brightest thing ever hung in earthly air, imperfect, erring, sinful are we all! Who of us will count ourselves among the mighty needing now no help? A perfect spirituality none will claim for himself, none will claim for his brother, none will claim for the saint he most enshrines and reveres. We all need some outward help; we all use for friendship and society and home, as well as for religion, some substantial symbol; we all ascend, if we ascend at all, some Jacob's ladder to the skies. Who ever flew thither save the Lord of glory himself? We all, therefore, should come to the table. A medium or mediator is requisite to us poor creatures clad in the flesh, tabernacled in clay, with the dust of our origin ever hanging about us; sometimes in our weariness and moral weakness feeling that we are all only dust, with nothing left of the living soul God breathed into Adam's nostrils, but to be completely resolved into the ashes whence we came! No symbol is so effectually adapted to our want as the Lord's Supper.

But whosoever personally and particularly the straying and lost sheep may be, and on however high or low a scale their demerit and frailty may be reckoned, for them unquestionably all means in religion are appointed, and why not this means especially, as well as all beside? We do not debar men from other instrumentalities of a religious sort because they are not yet distinctly numbered among the saints and favorites of the Great King, of which some of our hymns speak. Truly as the flowing lines in our sounding praise so characterize poor creatures not quite unlike ourselves, we shrink and wonder with a mixture of humor and alarm, while we query in our thought who are or can have been those thus described. Those of us consciously made of common earth, with a remnant of worldliness in us, the clay not worked out, if indeed any better than the wicked, are still seekers after all guidance and support. O, let us not dream yet of pretending to belong to a higher type in that moral kingdom embracing earth and heaven!

In fact, no other rite than the Lord's Supper is refused to any one. We do not forbid men to come to church and join in the devotions of the sanctuary because they are, or anybody should pronounce them, unrighteous. We do not say that Sunday, an institution most venerable of all, and somehow transmitted from the very foundations of human society, is too good for them to hallow in their use, and exists only for the elect. The most high and holy thing possible to man in the way of religious exercises and means, namely, spiritual communion with Almighty God, we enjoin upon the lowest of the vile.

I have referred already to that curiously instructive fact in Church history, of the Lord's Prayer, as now his Supper, being once forbidden to those considered imperfect. But, no longer daring to deny the former, shall we venture to refuse the latter? The present generation verily may see the countenance of its own exclusiveness in the mirror held up by the past, despise the past as it may.

Shall we withhold communion or the sign of communion with Jesus Christ, the Son of God, from all but such as have, to the satisfaction of an ecclesiastical tribunal, retraced their steps from the waste wilderness of sin to the garden and paradise of innocent joy? Shall we deny the prodigals any right of their hands and lips to this bread and wine? Do we then practise on the spirit of Christ's parable of transcendent pathos and beauty? If the slaves and victims of sensual appetite, whom Jesus himself did not curse or cast out, come and say, We think witnessing and partaking of this service will encourage us in our struggles to unloose the grasp of our deadly and inveterate foes, shall we venture to say to them, you shall not come? He that wrote with his finger on the ground, allowed the sinful woman to approach himself: shall we presume to send her away from his table? Is his table more sacred than his person? On what authority is the discrimination that singles out this from all the other means of religion, and turns it from a common privilege into a line between different classes of men? Certainly no word of Christ and no sentence of Scripture can be quoted in its behalf. It is an unauthorized ecclesiastical custom merely. Nor can that, with anything like respectable assumption of infallibility, be such a line, which some at least wicked Popes have consecrated, and on which bad men may stand and have stood. Even baptism, the other of the two peculiar rites of the Gospel, we administer to whosoever desires it for himself or his children. Why practise the inconsistency of shutting up the Supper? The first rite certainly demands for its condition as much faith and holy purpose as the latter.

I know the usage of the Church, in making the Supper a certificate of goodness or acceptance with God, has created an answering superstition among the people themselves, whose most common excuse for not sharing this rite is that they are not good enough. "I am not good enough," says the man who is invited to be a communicant. As if one were good in order to eat the Lord's Supper, instead of eating the Lord's Supper to be good! As if goodness were the means, and any outward ceremony the end! No, goodness for ever is the end, and all other things are but means to that. All other things are less mighty, less holy, less enduring in the sight of God and to the soul of man. Whatever spectacle can meet the eye, whatever sound fall upon the ear, and whatever act can be performed by the hands, are but beggarly elements in comparison. The eternal things are first and last, Alpha and Omega. All else is without, beneath, secondary, ministerial. All sights, accents, deeds, forms, however sanctified even by Jesus himself, come afterwards, and are inferior; for truly it is nothing less than absurd folly and treason against the Holy Ghost, to make any ceremony paramount to righteousness and truth. I am good, if good at all, for no collateral purpose in the world, — good with a view to nothing beyond being good. Not even in order to please God am I good, but to be like God, who, being goodness, makes goodness itself my object alone, to which everything else is instrumental. Even the Lord's Supper is but one of many means the Divine grace employs to subserve it. We partake that Supper, not because we are good, but that we may become so. Who that desires it for this result should not be allowed to partake it? We insist that men shall be Christians. How monstrous thus to insist, and at the same time deprive them of the very means that shall make them such!

In fine, by all this doctrine the dignity of

the Supper is not let down, but uplifted. To make any ordinance an end, would let down the human soul and the outward ordinance both together. For truly it were a poor object of the aspiration of an immortal being, to set before it any however solemn ceremony for its object and goal. But to make the ordinance a means is to give it a well-grounded and defensible grandeur, when we consider that for our growth in such things as a divine purity and love, in the revelation of Heaven's mercy, it stands, and to our human constitution is so fit. Thank God, that we can in such things flourish by any means! Therein, like the Apostle for the preaching of Christ, we do and will rejoice.

CHAPTER XIV.

ANALOGY.

As another argument for opening to the use of all every means of what we call revealed religion, the fact might be alleged that the means of natural religion are by God himself thus freely opened. There are means of religion in nature. Nature is not the soul's object, but minister, a mass of instruments and series of uses; and the frame of the universe is as religious as our own spiritual constitution. What seems most directly to relate to the body, is not exhausted in that relation, but has another and higher reference to the mind. As in the arts and convenient processes of life material must often, after its first application, be used over again, or its full value is not secured; so the whole creation, having met our senses, has with our sentiments a second sight and touch.

Accordingly the Gospel everywhere sets forth its spiritual truth under natural images. "Whosoever will, let him take the water of life freely," is its appeal. Certainly no declaration could throw the responsibility of being religious more clearly on ourselves. If the means of religion are free to everybody,—free as water, free as the river, the fountain, and the rain, to whosoever would drink,—he that is irreligious, without life and refreshment in his soul, is so not by any doom or curse, but like a man with lips parched when brooks are running through the valley, springs gushing from the hill-sides, showers pouring from the clouds; and to die of thirst is no necessity, but choice. No distinction or exception is made, as to the various means of religion, of some one that may be used by particular persons, and by others not. Bible or Sunday, closet or public worship, baptism or Supper, sermon, song, conversation, prayer, — any, all the means,— whatsoever can be water of life to a human soul, reviving in it the spirit of love and obedience to God,—use whosoever will! It is so in the system of nature. And the point of Scrip-

Accordingly the Gospel everywhere sets forth its spiritual truth under natural images. "Whosoever will, let him take the water of life freely," is its appeal. Certainly no declaration could throw the responsibility of being religious more clearly on ourselves. If the means of religion are free to everybody, — free as water, free as the river, the fountain, and the rain, to whosoever would drink, — he that is irreligious, without life and refreshment in his soul, is so not by any doom or curse, but like a man with lips parched when brooks are running through the valley, springs gushing from the hill-sides, showers pouring from the clouds; and to die of thirst is no necessity, but choice. No distinction or exception is made, as to the various means of religion, of some one that may be used by particular persons, and by others not. Bible or Sunday, closet or public worship, baptism or Supper, sermon, song, conversation, prayer, — any, all the means, — whatsoever can be water of life to a human soul, reviving in it the spirit of love and obedience to God, — use whosoever will! It is so in the system of nature. And the point of Scrip-

bloom of the earth, beyond your board or shop or granary, is properly, and was by God designed for, a means of religion, of exciting grateful admiration for the infinite bounty and beauty. How much of the glory can we buy or sell, devour or wear? All the rest is for religion, worship, thanks to Him who provides not only for the perishing animal, but the immortal mind. The sun, that lights up the scene,—is it a mere illuminator of the earth, a burning reflector, only larger than our hand-lamp and broader than the blaze from the headland? If our soul, while our body rides over the earth, never rode in its flaming chariot to God, are we better or worse than the Persian worshipper of the sun itself? Truly, as a means of religion, it can be used by all. The poorest drunkard that staggers by the way can climb up into its celestial seat, if he will. Better worship the sun itself than worship nothing! Better, indeed, worship God in and through the sun, in all its brightness but his shadow! Ah, yonder rolling and shining, it is a means of religion, not to all, but, among all the millions, to whosoever will.

The sea, doubtless, may be contemplated by us in a wholly utilitarian way. So it is contemplated by most persons. Why not? Such is its obvious character! It is a well from which the sunbeams and winds are drawers, distillers, and common carriers to our cups and fields. It is a liquid floor or bridge, across which our ships convey passengers and goods for the society, commerce, exchanges, and wealth of mankind. It is a great refriger ator and briny purifier of the air. It is a store of medicine, doing more with its salubrity than all other medicines to preserve health keep off disease, and prolong life. All this, in a utilitarian way, doubtless it is. But, blaz ing there with the dawn, brooded over by the night, that settles down over it so dun and black, does it make us kindle or shudder with no such sense of the Presence Infinite and Eternal as once bore the sceptical poet By ron on the wings of his imagination for a while so above the lowness of his doubt and contempt, that he wrote the grandest religious ode to the sea all literature, ancient or modern out of the Bible, can present? Truly it too beyond all our Protestant or Catholic sectarianism, is a means of religion to every soul it can touch.

As a particular illustration, behold that billow, a monster that travels before the fury of the storm, stirring the ocean's heart for a thousand miles, looming up dim and huge as your eye first notes it advancing to the shore, turning its perfect arch as solid masonry from the unstable drops, thinning the bulk of its tremendous base to a falchion-like edge, poised gleaming and quivering, unbroken till the opposite wind blows off its delicate top into spray, which the setting western beam changes to rainbows that line the awful, gloomy ridge with charms of incomparable richness, transferring Heaven's covenant of mercy after the deluge from the tempestuous driving rack above to the misty surface of the angry deep, as though God's sign of mercy must surmount and clothe everything high or low; till the magnificent, momentary structure breaks with a roaring in the ear long-resounding through the air, which you know not whether to call transcendently soft, or infinitely loud, — as it were the voice of Spirit: what use will you make of it, to what purpose convert it, if not to wonder and adore? According to the analogy I am pursuing, it is a means of religion free for all, who with any pious sensibility observe or conceive it, to use; as I argue every Christian means should be used.

No means of religion without us, yea, in the land and the sun and the sea! No God to be seen and adored in nature, when so remarkably in two seasons of disaster, separated by a score of years, the overruling Power has made the winter days, with slight and short exceptions, so gentle to his impoverished children, "tempering the wind to the shorn lamb"! We may see nothing but accident, chance, and matter, instead of a Providence, in the wheels of nature and the hairs of our head. We may count and use this great world of God as a staging for our play, a couch for our self-indulgence, a market for our gain. But regarding and employing it thus alone, we pervert or confine it to its narrowest end.

It has been argued that the stars must be inhabited, because *what else are they good for?* Save only a few of them,—such as the pole-star that shows to the sailor, and to the night-wanderer or fugitive, the north; and Jupiter's moons, by their eclipses marking the vessel's place; and some other centres or satellites that help us lay our courses or sketch our charts and maps,—of what small profit in their pale lustre are they all! the result, how insignificant to the outlay, reduced to a guide-board or signal for a surveyor's glass! Not so I reason this question of their use. Hung yonder on nothing, in boundless ether, keeping to their punctual tracks, closer than the vulture's eye could follow, or, too distant to be distinctly descried, fading off into that Milky-Way which points to yet unseen and inconceivably constellated grandeur, what are they, and what are they meant for, but a means of religion wide as the world?

If, in this connection, at the risk of being thought childish and trivial, I may venture to allude to a phenomenon so enchanting, yet elusive,—there is one piece of the scenery of his universe, which God shows us more rarely than sun or sea or stars, as though to arouse us by its strangeness and infrequency, as well as wondrous splendor. Unlike things I have already noticed, it is no means of gross and common utility at all, and has nothing to do with our housekeeping or husbandry. No such thing can be made of it. We cannot breathe it like the air, or be directed by it as the light. The sun is a ripener of the corn, as well as shadow of the Deity; the sea is a bond between nations, as it is an image of immensity; the mountains are sources of streams, while altars of the Most High; and the stars are candles over the dusky deep, no less than illustrations of the handiwork of God. But of this enigma and magnificent riddle what can we make? Once in a great while its unique figure comes flashing out in the northerly heavens, changing before we can fix the spot of its origin, and perhaps, ere we can challenge a companion's regard to some matchless point in its amazing exhibition, vanishing away.

Yes, Aurora at midnight, a dawn in the

dark, a second singular sort of morning fleeting and wandering, as out of place, among the risen orbs! Neither guide nor purifier is it, fountain nor nourisher, lantern nor bridge, — nothing useful, or available, as we say, — only a piece of heaven's curtain rather, dropped down into earthly air, falling from some angel's loosened hand during the moment of his diverted mind, part of the tapestry of the New Jerusalem, waving awhile over our planet to show us how those upper palace-walls are hung; or something like this gathering of gleaming ranks, into which it is so soon converted, looked not the celestial troop that once marched and sang over the fields of Palestine? Was not this the bright pennon which lured on the first Roman imperial convert, Constantine, to our religion, in that story told of him, with its sign of victory? In rapid turns advancing and retreating, 'tis a holy dance of ghostly creatures, with indescribable grace circling and gliding, and ineffable glory in the pure pallor of their pearly forms. But, while we question, to our instant gazing they change their robes, woven of no imaginable stuff or texture, to tints of green or rosy flushes, as though warm, substantial existences. Our friends departed, in their seraphic shapes, are they not? Surely more seemly thus than in some other supposed apparitions! Once more, the almost living motions become a shape of massive and dead architecture, a solid wall of sharp or re-entering angles, as though fort or castle were built in the skies. Yet soon all melts away, — nothing but blank space and emptiness left in the region where shone from God sublimity beyond snowy peaks and foaming cataracts; and we cannot follow its trail, trace one step of its going more than of its coming, discern its producing cause or terrestrial effect.

What is it? What is it for? Materialist, sceptic scorner, is it a mere levity and vanity of God, unworthy the minute for description I give it, and fitly treated in its spectral apparition and flight with our hasty and purely worldly glance? Science staggers at the sight, talks vaguely of polar ice, electric agency, and changing weather, as floats off the splendid mockery of its curious conjecturing eye. Is it then all for naught? No, to revering minds it is a means of religion, pure revelation, clean from heaven, a sacred architecture indeed beyond Gothic arches for our aspirations, finely useless to our coarser wants, that in every particle and movement it may feed and stir our nobler faculties, and, in lofty soaring, tempt our thoughts its own celestial way to Him who suspends and then withdraws his banner in the skies. It is gross to be heedless of the beauty in his creation God displays, and irreligious to rest in it as mere material beauty. What curse or doom keeps us from reaching God even over these light stairs, and out of this very gossamer weaving a wedding-garment for our souls? Whosoever will, in this or any spectacle of the creation, note the rustle and glitter of the vesture of God passing by, as he passed by Moses beneath the Mount, shall have his devotion enlivened to the Author of his being and Ordainer of his lot. Not like a human display, not to please prince or favorite, is His drapery ever blown abroad; to be no private exhibition in a closed room for nobility or money, is the cunning web of nature unrolled from the loom of heaven, quickly to be unravelled as in a dream; for no solitary soul alone to ascend, is its Jacob's ladder set up, — for it is still set up, only Jacob saw it and we may not, — but for who ever has sensibility to the beauty that God delights in, to rise by, and, as he rises, to learn that what seems most vain for worldly ends may lift us above this dusty spot, until — and would it were oftener! —

> "We're lost in wonder, love, and praise."

Just so it is with all the means of religion we call revealed, — the doctrines, precepts, ordinances, influences, times and places, forms and exercises, of the Gospel of Christ. Whosoever will may have and use them. *One* man *wills*, another will *not*. To one man the mountain is a shrine; to another, it is but something in his way. To one man's thinking, elemental forces alone of fire and flood determine the proportions of land and sea; another sees the finger of God marking the line whose finest sand the waters may not pass. One man sees the lesser globes scaling off from the larger in their circling flight, or condensing from dark nebulæ into luminous balls; and another notes the hand of Divinity loosing the sweet influences of Pleiades, binding the bands of Orion, and guiding Arcturus with his sons; and three thousand years of improvement in science and literature have not been able to add to the description one single touch! So one man finds in the Bible priestly pretension, politic calculation, human composition; and another the inspiration of the Holy Ghost for the salvation of the human soul, "water of life" flowing from the time of Jacob's first patriarchal well to Christ's talk with the woman of Samaria.

The beauty of nature thus answers to the grace of God. What abundant provision God has made for such beauty, unserviceable save for the spirit,—beauty that tempts not the woodman's axe or the reaper's sickle,—beauty that can be gathered into no barns, carried for export or exchange with foreign countries by no fleets, woven into no robes, cut and polished into no engines,—beauty that can be bought and sold for no price, but the property of everybody who can see it, — beauty of blossom and wild-flower, that no scythe is sharp and hungry for, no rumbling wain can take its load of, and no agent for wool or flax or grain travels to barter, — beauty that cannot be spun, as Jesus tells us the lilies themselves do not spin, — beauty that will not furnish manure for the ground, ornament for the person, condiment or viand for the board, and yield neither sugar nor starch, silk nor fur, flour nor spice, — beauty which is no road but direct indeed to a higher country, and no clothing save of God, but is offered freely to every human soul!

Is the Gospel on another plan? No, devout or undevout as men may be before nature or the grace of God, in his works, — unless all instances and illustrations, such as I have adduced, be in vain, — he undeniably opens the means of religion to all his rational creatures. On short allowance or in utter destitution of bread and water, the body may by land or sea be placed; but there is always something for the hunger and thirst that is within.

Christianity corresponds with nature in this regard. The draughts of this world's pleasure may leave our lips parched, and the doctrines of its philosophy fail to satisfy the craving of our hearts; how blest that we can still come to the supplies of God!

CHAPTER XV.

CRISIS.

THE plan of making the Lord's Supper as open as public prayer and praise, is resisted on the ground that thus we should lose our mark of the great religious crisis in human life. This particular and most important use of the Supper, which it has subserved and still so widely promotes in the Church, it may be said, takes it out of that general analogy I have run; for there is nothing in nature to which this part of revelation can correspond.

Acknowledging the propriety of considering this question more thoroughly than its occurrence among other points in a former connection allowed, I yet feel how greatly its discussion is perplexed by the quite diverse foundations of faith on which alike this practical office of the Lord's table is proposed and maintained. By persons taking the same stand, the nature of the crisis would indeed be variously described, and based on different theories of the soul. The common psychology assumes a total depravity at birth, from which, at one or another period of growing and adult years, through the sudden pleasure of God working by his Spirit and the faith of his Son, individuals of his offspring are delivered into the number of saints elect in light and love. A more liberal school of theology assumes that man in his native state has no moral or spiritual character, but, by the Divine providence and grace being brought to the unfolding of a higher nature, is in Scripture phrase born again, — or that, having degenerated from childish innocence, and lost all original righteousness, and wandered into every way of selfishness and sin, he is redeemed from his iniquity, crosses the line which separates the corrupt from the pure, and so passes from death unto life. In either case, personal participation in the Lord's Supper is thought the proper signal of changes or events so great. Some reasoners on the subject prefer to present partaking of the Supper in the light of a conscientious will, as a religious profession or distinct taking before men of the Lord's side, and a resolution to live by his commands. But this implies of course the same inward transformation, and makes the table the same line between those who have passed and the rest who have not reached the crisis supposed. Still again, by increasing numbers of such as would be at once liberal and just to every sober or ghastly fact of human life, a mixed doctrine is set forth, of human nature as neither innocent nor utterly impure, yet coming into the world under some curse of Adam, if not of God, and needing to reach a grand turning-point and pass through a swift revolution to be saved. To contemplate the conflict of the most orthodox on this or any other article, is to think always of something like the figure a friend of mine humorously offered, of a company of foxes with the brushes of their tails indeed beautifully together, but their heads in every direction of the compass!

But the inquiry must be met. Is there universally or generally, among those becoming God's true children and Christ's faithful followers, such a crisis and definable moment in their internal history, from which, as from a mountain-top, on the side behind all flows backward, and all forward on that before? and is this particular commemoration of Jesus legitimately chosen to identify that line?

Unquestionably we must admit the fact of crises in all nature and life. Let all be growth, cry some, growth in the soul as in the vegetable world. But all is not growth without us; why therefore within? There is a law of change as well as of development. The humblest plant, as has been well said, has crises, no less than slow expansions, in its history. The germ swells till it bursts the perhaps tough covering of the seed that was sown, it may be breaks the seed itself in two, pierces the ground to reach the light; and though there is gradation, as the Master teaches, yet are not the degrees so many crises,—"first the blade, then the ear, after that the full corn in the ear"? Truly are there many images of the soul's critical unfolding. Behold them in the body natural and the body politic, in the progress of disease in an organized frame and the morbid and healthy states of a community, nay, in the most petty business that attains to the dignity and calculation of a scheme! The great poet of our race only tells its experience when he says, "There is a tide in the affairs of men."

But the question is whether there be in the soul's biography one particular crisis, diverse from and exceeding all others, through which, in its unmistakable sameness, every rational creature must go on his way to the kingdom of God, and whether the Lord's Supper is the true and warranted signal thereof.

Truly on no question is it more difficult to be positive, or wrong to dogmatize, than on at least the first of these. It is comfortable to the mind to believe in regular stages, in progress out of evil, and in the perseverance of the saints. In the creation all Scripture records and scientific observations show that God himself proceeded in the way of orderly advance. Not creeping, but stepping, behold him at his work! His universe is a series of new, successive productions of perfect wisdom and will. But internal scrutiny of creative processes in the soul is harder to make. Beside, we are peculiarly liable to deception in comparing our present with our past. We think the last performance of true genius the finest we ever saw, our latest vivid emotion the strongest we ever felt, as the sailor may tell us the last surge was the highest ever surmounted by his ship. Who can relatively measure the waves on the sea of life!

The most distinguished of our natural historians has lately written a great essay on classification of the animal kingdom. But spiritual classification is the most baffling sort we can undertake. Minerals, plants, and to a great degree animals, can be classified by external characteristics, and visible, sensible, material habits. But to put moral natures in rows higher and lower is no such easy task. The very agent in this classification is none other than the very Spirit of God. That bloweth like the wind. It is immeasurable as the atmosphere. It is very hard indeed to catch in its swift, invisible movements. We cannot know in any superficial way what hearts it has visited, nor, without an angel's eye, could we always see into what hearts it is making its way. In the smallest church and in the whole world alike, where it has touched, how impossible for us absolutely to decide! It alone fully knows its own doings and can tell its own story. It truly is a self-registering instrument or power of the Most High. Yet nevertheless its action in raising and sanctifying the minds of men how abundantly great and evident in the world!

But as respects the persons it has affected, been repelled from, or passed by, to call them by name, run lines of discrimination and set up barriers of demarcation, is to run the risk of injustice to them and it together. No flashes of other light are equal to its gleams; no earthly workings are mighty as its deeds. So much can we say, yet hesitate to mark once for all the individuals through whom they appear, so wonderfully alterable they are in this respect of revealing the Holy One, now visited and anon seeming abandoned by the Spirit,—perhaps like David sinking back into unworthiness and sin after his harp had rung and his voice burst into unquestionably inspired jubilees of praise! With such falls from grace and such leaps of virtue in this goodness of God, who shall be surveyors of metes and bounds of particular ownership in the moral territory? Who shall be the assessors on the variable amounts of this unseen property and treasure of the heart? Truly do we not need, over and above church committees, an apostolic succession to decide for this? Nay, beyond even that general succession, a transmission of the special miraculous gift of "discerning of spirits," would be required. Where, then, are the functionaries who can authenticate their title of being clothed with this rare and exalted power? Where, in any actual passing upon the sheep and goats, are the results of its exercise so clear and satisfactory that nobody can dispute or be fairly grieved by the award? The truth is, all attempts by a formal badge or fence to distinguish precisely the lost from the saved have proved such failures, at least so rude and often illusive, as to show that God never intended they should by any concert of ecclesiastical factors or construction of church machinery be made. They are like the walls the Chinese and the Romans made in their several provinces to keep out the savages of the North. The savages got over the walls, and demonstrated themselves how often as good and honest folks as they who had branded them as barbarians and held them at arm's length!

If a charge of unfaithfulness be brought against those declining or opposing this prerogative of deciding between the characters of men by a formal test, none is more exposed to it than the Master himself! He disallowed and assailed every such test; he made the street as holy as the synagogue; he cared nothing for outer or inner courts, for Jew or Gentile; he found the blood of Abraham in no direct line of fleshly descent, but in whatever heart beat with the sentiment of Abraham's faith; he turned hill-sides and shores into altars and pulpits; he knew as well as we how rarely ecclesiastical bars dispense a just award!

That those who have with punctual fidelity observed the exercises and ordinances of the Christian religion, have proved on the whole the best disciples of Jesus, I will not deny, but rather in the probability of such a fact cordially believe. That the wickedness and apostasy of mankind from God are so general and great as to require manifold and mighty agencies, — not only the pleadings of God's voice and the sufferings of his Son, but wise expedients and every sort of machinery even, whose wheels a finger of God may anywise touch and move, to rescue wandering souls from imminent ruin, — I sorrowfully yet distinctly confess. But the vehement doubt is, whether within the general body of disciples the selection of a particular rite, to single out his chosen friends from those less good and religious, has not in all ages been greatly fallacious, and is not now more fallacious than ever. The reason is, sanctity itself resents this method. In saying, by our general belief, custom, and worship, that we are Christians, and not Pagans, Mohammedans, or Mormons, there is of course no pretension or assumption of an invidious sort. It is an outward or general classification. It is a geographical boundary. It is a doctrinal peculiarity. But to determine, by a manifest ritual touchstone, who among the nominal Christians are real, is not only going further, but in a different line, nay, in a direction so offensive to a refined and delicate mind, that with all its might it withstands, or with all its speed escapes, the experiment. The disciples will not stay to be counted. Like tender doves, the fearful birds of heaven, they fly from the lifted finger of our arithmetic. It is only the flock of duller earth-bound creatures that are quite content to be reckoned and stamped or labelled. Yet with all this the servants and soldiers of the Lord are not a quite unknown or invisible troop, but loyal in every emergency, and ready whenever the good fight of faith is to be fought. When Christ's name is abused with contempt, or his cause checked by opposition, the courage to honor and serve him in word and deed is one thing, and quite aside from the complacent admitting of an imputation of friendship for him, made or accepted that we may be praised and glorified among the lights of the world and the heirs of heaven. That which is the leaven does not boast or show itself, but hides, diffusing its virtue through the whole lump. That which is really the salt of the earth does not like to be called so, unless indeed by the Saviour himself. Keenly, too, as any one may penetrate the secret sphere of motive and feeling in others' breasts, he finds himself, if not frequently mistaken, yet not seldom making discoveries in those he thought he had already known.

Supposing, however, the classification feasible, a question would arise upon the authority or propriety of making the Lord's Supper, in the way so usual, of all other modes or rites, its great and peculiar term. I must deny that such was its first intention, or can be its proper use. Not to distinguish between, nay, but on the contrary to unite, disciples of the widest grades of worth, loyalty, and spirituality, so that the better might sanctify the worse, was the evident, blessed genius and purpose in Christ's own mind of its institution. In the appointment or request of Christ, in the Acts of the Apostles, and in the first ages, so far as we can penetrate their obscurity, of the early Church, there is no hint of its being designed or employed as a measuring-rod of individual graces, or, in the reverse construction, as a rod to scourge delinquent pupils in the Christian school; and only after some centuries had passed, do we read oi mere beginners in that school being sent away from the table, at which those having learnt or being supposed to understand, the lesson: more perfectly, were allowed to stay.

Moreover, were it right at all to make th Supper such a signal, it would still remain t be queried whether it should be a signal t man or to God. Every act and ordinance o religion is, and should be, to God a signal o sincerity and obedient love. The extent t which it is not so, is always and exactly th gauge of our hypocrisy. But a signal hel out to man, to our fellow-believer or fellow creature, for comparison of ourselves with ot ers not arrived at the point where, like th banner of an army, we display it to hint th length of our march, has a quite alien sens and quality. I cannot read that Jesus cou selled or permitted any such signal. He pr vided no material index of our piety. He to!

us not to point with any forefinger of our own at our good deserts of faith or duty. O, far better the unconscious signals, the involuntary testimonies of excellence he held forth, and his followers in all their appearance and demeanor cannot but exhibit! Every formal signal of holiness is naught. It has about it a somewhat pharisaic savor, from which it can scarcely be freed. It is like the long prayer, or the devout posture at the corner of the streets, or the broad phylactery of the law on the forehead, or any other peculiar sign or advertisement of religion, which may be consistent with the immorality of excessive pride, sensual impurity, or fraudulent devouring of widow's houses. The Supper, exhibited as such a standard of mutual comparison or self-comparison, is put to a use against which must arise the threefold charge of its being unintended by Jesus, intrinsically inappropriate or unadapted, and, in itself, essentially wrong, — that is to say, a use which not this ordinance, or anything in the nature of a punctual form, should, or can rightfully, promote.

The question of a crisis, of course, is distinct from that of the manner in which any crisis existing should be signalized. But I apprehend it is not a question to be decided one way by any Church for the race as a whole. Human nature has been handled with this rough indiscriminateness long enough! Every sect, of repute more or less evangelical, is getting tired of an estimate so vague and rude. All thought and all fact agree in shaming and discouraging the old monotonous descriptions of the human soul as in every breast an invariable thing. We must not only speak of man, but of men; in spiritual, though not ecclesiastical judgment, greatly distinguishing one from another, as God and Christ themselves, contrary to all speculations of equal merit or demerit among moral creatures, so plainly aver that they do. What thousands, in the strictest orders bound by the severest creeds, deny the power to fix in memory, or assert with truth, any imagined chronological instant of salvation! I have heard the most pious leader in the most austere band declare, if his redemption depended on any such hasty experience, he must, past all hope, be lost. It is not necessary to go to Baxter or John Newton for evidence. All around us are witnesses without number to the gentle coming, opening, and ripening of all that is precious in human character, as of the light, the flower, and the fruit. But yesterday a man, whose soul is a perpetual flame of fervor in devotion, assured me he had always loved God, and that there never was a time when he was not averse from the wicked; and the grass has grown green for many a season over the grave of a woman, who affirmed to her friends that the great Power never appeared to her, from her first recollection, other than as a Father. These may be rare instances. Many more, doubtless, are the instances where conviction of sin, overturning of the mind, a crisis between destruction and life, a clear and open exchange of sorrow for joy, with transaction as marked as in any worldly account, denotes the great experiment of the soul. Nevertheless, He that looks down upon the generations of men sees, and for the future foresees, not conversion, but education, as the hereditary religious law. One crisis is therefore not to be affirmed as alike needful for all; but, in our reckoning making men neither better nor worse than they are, let us consider all opinions of human nature dangerous, not as they are more or less favorable, but only as they are not true to every case.

If, in fine, it be alleged that the tendency of these remarks is to destroy or confound distinctions, I must plead, it is not real, but only certain conventional distinctions, with which they are meant so to deal. Jesus Christ did away with nominal and formal distinctions, but only that vital ones might appear. It is not against distinctions themselves that any thoughtful man could speak, but only against particular methods of making them, or against putting the hollow and fictitious in place of the solid and deep. Distinctions, in the very nature of things, are ordained by God. Verily it is not quite necessary we should make them; for they are already made! It is not possible we should destroy, or, by any wicked will or wit of ours, expose ourselves to the objection preferred. The worst man may disregard spiritual distinctions, but cannot annihilate them.

Admirable spectacle, for men to wonder and angels to smile at, any attempt to obliterate differences in human character and kind! Let him moved by such ambition try first to erase or even smooth over the diversities of lower nature. *Species cannot be confounded*, is a fundamental maxim with the scientific naturalist, against the modern heresy that any one thing or creature can grow out of another. Nature has boundaries stricter than those of kingdoms, more immovable than the Romans fancied of the station of their god Terminus. I have seen the brier clasp some solid trunk and weave its tendrils and leaves through the branches of the pine to its top; but the brier was brier in every thorn and leaf, and the pine was itself in every one of the green needles of which Nature makes her sweetest wind-harp in the world. I have seen the oak, the ash, and the birch, three lofty trees, seemingly rising from one root, so closely were they joined from the very ground. But I knew, without looking, it was not one root, because Nature never so mixes her living substances, but keeps every special atom and fibre after its kind and

heard of,—he will distinguish himself. So a man of any genuine type of Christian excellence will distinguish himself more than could any pope, meeting of inquisitors, college of cardinals, distinguish him. He will and does very successfully distinguish himself in every deed he does, word he speaks, tone of his voice, and look of his countenance. It is his deed, word, tone, look, and that of no other in the world; and sooner shall one of the inferior animals pass for another, the lion be mistaken for the lamb,—though the predicted time may come for them to lie down together,—than the two opposite human dispositions obscure or be merged in one another.

The ordinance of the Supper, then, cannot properly be employed as a test severing the righteous from the sinful; for it is the use and office of no ordinance whatsoever to do this. They will do this sufficiently for themselves. The substances of oil and water will not mix better, or part more decisively, for any order issued or ceremony performed; and what more "concord hath Christ with Belial, or a believer with an infidel"? We are altogether super-

heard of,—he will distinguish himself. So a man of any genuine type of Christian excellence will distinguish himself more than could any pope, meeting of inquisitors, college of cardinals, distinguish him. He will and does very successfully distinguish himself in every deed he does, word he speaks, tone of his voice, and look of his countenance. It is his deed, word, tone, look, and that of no other in the world; and sooner shall one of the inferior animals pass for another, the lion be mistaken for the lamb,—though the predicted time may come for them to lie down together,—than the two opposite human dispositions obscure or be merged in one another.

The ordinance of the Supper, then, cannot properly be employed as a test severing the righteous from the sinful; for it is the use and office of no ordinance whatsoever to do this. They will do this sufficiently for themselves. The substances of oil and water will not mix better, or part more decisively, for any order issued or ceremony performed; and what more "concord hath Christ with Belial, or a believer with an infidel"? We are altogether super-

16

serviceable when we undertake to draw over again the lines which Nature drew with her mighty finger ere parallels or meridians were traced on the colored map, or shores and seas painted on an artificial globe. Nor need our weak finger follow that of the Almighty to finish its work, as it trenches deep betwixt love and hatred, reverence and blasphemy, sincerity and hypocrisy, in the human soul. The shades of character are too delicate, and its springs too subtile and profound, for most persons precisely to define or fathom ; nor can we believe there ever existed a *company* of men competent and wise enough for the work. In other words, accurate ecclesiastical judgment is impossible. It is not judgment, but ignorance or error. Universities and courts give degrees and titles of honor, and run great risks and commit great blunders as they do it. Far more difficult to make the decree fair between the upright and the ungodly. It will be made without our help. Christ's true Church will not be confounded with the world, however the pretended one may be, until the world becomes his Church, and we judge no more, but only know and love each other.

CHAPTER XVI.

WHOLENESS.

INDIVIDUAL members of the Church will have many a crisis, and perhaps some one great crisis, in their personal religious life; but any line, formally drawn between those supposed to have passed through and those understood not to have experienced such a crisis, actually wounds the unity and destroys the wholeness of the body. From Rome, a thousand miles away to Ephesus, about a church with its centre near a thousand miles farther still, at Jerusalem, planted to run and grow through divisions of Hebrew prejudice, Pagan idolatry, and polytheistic worship, Paul writes that "there is one body." He tells the Galatians that in Christ is neither Jew nor Greek, bond nor free, male nor female; and repeats to the Corinthians, that there are many members, but one grand whole. Alas! how far even yet are we from the fact he asserts! We are very congratulatory that the soldiers rent not Christ's robe; but what cares he for his cast-off garment, compared with the living body of his followers, which scarce any one hesitates to tear!

Beautiful, confessedly, as the idea of this unity is, many will continue to say, in the diversities of human constitution and character, it is impracticable. I answer, it was practised by Christ himself. Were there ever greater varieties, sharper inconsistencies, than in the little band of his first adherents, which *he* nevertheless kept together with him on earth? The meditative, loving John; the forward, hasty, passionate Peter, with the ventures and excitements of the fishery still in his manner; the cool and sceptical Thomas, a free-thinker of *those* times; the calculating, historic Matthew, the ring of the tax-gatherer's table in his ears; the moralizing James; the comparatively neutral figures in the group; even the miserly Judas, with his bag held till at the last crisis he diabolically withdrew himself;—who but Jesus could have kept such varieties of worth and demerit together, till, with real cause for exultation, he could say to his Father, "Those thou hast given me I have kept, — none lost but the son of perdition"; so that the Twelve, as they are proverbially called, are the only numerical company ever on earth that shall go down undissolved and indissoluble in human imagination to the "last syllable of recorded time." Nay, to what does the traitor, Iscariot, owe the final touch of grace and repentance, with which he acknowledged his betrayal of "the innocent blood," and would have come back to the old relation, but to a feeling he could not hush, of that wonderful Being's love and patience to bear with him, take him along, toil to teach and train him, and never expel or excommunicate him, though he clung a spy to his side, or sat an incarnate, embodied hypocrisy at his board? Not impracticable, then, is the doctrine of one Body of Christ's votaries, unless Christ's example is impracticable alike with his *word.*

But why insist on this unity? Wherefore should Paul care for it, or Christ care for it, or we care for it? Because, I reply, it is a principle of all life and goodness, — even the most vital and central point in our religion. Because unity, not alone in an ecclesiastical fellowship, but universally in any body of persons, is the indispensable condition of harmony and health. Disunity everywhere is disease, dissolution. Do we not all know it is necessary, for example, a family should be one body, to be happy? Different sexes, ages, relations, talents, callings, are embraced in one household. Yet if all the individuals, young and old, do not make one body in the communion of a good understanding and the perfection of a loving spirit, what discord, disease, is in the dwelling! Only when any body of related persons has unity, can it have sanity or health. Sickness in the natural frame of the human body, inflammation, ague, arises how? When some one part refuses its function. If in heart, lungs, brain, any organ, there is no action, and it does not play and do its proper part with the rest, then all is diseased. Alas! in how many families are colds and fevers, — not produced by the weather, not affecting the physical organs, but continuing all the time! It is lack of unity. A keen observer perceives it as he enters a domestic circle, as certainly as he would notice a hectic color or a cough. The child does not want to do the parent's bidding; while, from the rebellious assurance, or the cunning fret, it is plain this is no rare occurrence, but a chronic difficulty, of an unsweetened temper and an unsubdued will. The parents discuss questions in others' presence with a latent heat it is not hard to imagine breaking out behind their visitor's back, or which he hears breaking out while he knocks at the door. A low, dull pain, as of a grumbling tooth, pervades the sensibilities of those by their vow, according to the Scripture, made "one flesh." Brothers and sisters, in the homely phrase, pull different ways, till it becomes a continual problem whether there is affection enough left to prevent the secret alienation from ending in visible rupture and open hate. Do we think this disunited, unhealthy state of the domestic body is not written plainly in our faces, and audible clearly in our voices, wherever it exists? Ay, as plainly as any disease of our flesh! The uncomfortable atmosphere of our home chills everybody that comes into it. We cannot change the social temperature at a momentary wish, or by any wilful concealments, more than we could make the mercury in the thermometer on our mantelpiece rise without change in the air. We imagine that being on our guard, or on our good behavior, for the hour some friend or caller is with us under our roof, hides our jealousies, or want of mutual love and want of unity, from all our acquaintance. But somehow, mysteriously, our dislike or indifference is discerned and known. The very aspect of things reveals it. The dead furniture we handle together turns state's evidence. Every article strangely speaks of love in a happy, that is, a united family, "one body"; — how soft and kind the unity makes everything even inanimate! It gets into the very chairs and books as they are passed, and is heard in the opening and shutting of the doors; or else everything reports the antipathy, and lets out the hidden anger and distrust. The table we sit at, while we sit about it and speak and gaze across it, shows whether the circle is complete, more than it could by all the marvellous raps and strange motions which, to some, indicate a supernatural presence. It divulges to every quick observer and hearer the moral secrets of our heart and nature, which we thought locked from all human knowledge. Not unseen is the skeleton, said to be in every mansion and every bosom. You may be *smooth-faced;* but you could not look thus and so, as you do sometimes, at one you loved with all your heart. You may be smooth-tongued before folks for the most part; but what means that sharp tone that escapes as from prison in your breast, and makes you blush at the recoil, as though you had disclosed something that ought to be wrapped up? It, and everything like it, means the want in the body domestic of that unity which makes the family, in some cases, the most glorious, as it is the oldest institution, grander than any royalty, republic, league of enterprise, letters, science, in the world.

"*There is one Body,*" — in every tie that

binds persons together, it is God's everlasting statute. Unity of sentiment and aim is the absolute requisite for any soundness or lasting peace. It is as true in civil as in religious applications. Why has it taken all the vitality of our popular principles to accommodate in one governmental system this local matter of slavery, inevitably compromised as an inheritance of the past in our constitution, of which we have found it yet impossible to get rid? A case not for surgery, lest the patient bleed to death, yet yielding so slowly to alterative medicines, why is it our obstinate national thorn in the flesh? Because it is an alien element, marring the unity of our body politic. Why are peak and valley far west in our domain now amazed at our suddenly unfurled banners, and bristling with our arms ready to wage a half-civil war? Because an ill fester of polygamy on one limb, a territorial member of our confederacy, cannot be confined to that single spot, but sends a thrill of anguish thousands of miles through all our borders, even to wave-washed Florida, and Maine, the State of pines, and divides that unity of our political body without which it cannot be well in health.

The whole Body literally means the same thing as the well Body. Any wounding or severing is malady alike in the corporeal organization and the social frame. "There is one Body";—and in the most insignificant, temporary, and transient body of persons, with all the variety of tendencies and tastes, there must be also some comprehensive unity, or it will be at cross purposes, with distress and defeat.

Take even a travelling party for example,—if I may be suffered to use so simple an illustration. Thus not unfrequently it happens one wishes to take this route, and another that; the first prefers land-carriage, and the second water; this enthusiast thinks natural scenery the great object, and that works of art; and opinions still further subdivide upon the comparative attractions of great architectural buildings, palaces, and cathedrals, or galleries and museums of pictures, statuary, manuscripts, and books; while the main anxiety of a considerable proportion of the migratory troop is to reach the best inns and revel in the most luxurious living of meats and drinks while they are afoot. As each section pushes against the others its choice, there will be small pleasure in the journey, as ten thousand companies that started merrily in stage or steamer have discovered, because there is no unity in the body. So everywhere in all things. The obscurest friendship, the noisiest club, the most numerous association, must have unity, or it is on the point of breaking up and destruction.

We consider it a point of little concern whether the body ecclesiastic, in its form and custom, be two or one. Is it of trivial moment whether your business-firm have unity or not? May one of the partners determine the policy, conclude the contract, privately use and affix the signature, without consulting or apprising the rest, — and all this to the promoting of your commercial prosperity? Will there be no loss, waste, and failure in this disunion and want of concert? Does not the old fable of the *bundle of rods* — weak when parted, strong when joined — agree with *Paul's creed* and Christ's prayer that the only health or security is in "One Body"? Then it is no trifle whether or not we make one body in Christ. Unity is important and indispensable; it is health, peace, and salvation, in a house, in a shop, in a journey, in a partnership, in society: but not in religion? Ah! one of the vulgar names of Satan, the Devil himself, means simply *two!*

Ye that would save the union of the county, keep union in the Church also. We may be assembled, yet not united. We are not one body because one building holds us, any more than different persons are one by abiding under the same roof, meeting in the same counting-room, travelling in the same coach, when they may be at swords' points. But we are one only when the faith and love of the Gospel bind us together. Let Unitarians, as they are called, be such in no party sense or merely theological one respecting a single doctrine of the Divine nature, but in the sense, from Christ's prayer and Paul's creed, of the one Body. Parish, society, congregation, church, whatever the name, let that which is named, through all distinctions of belief, be one thing alone.

But if all compose the unity, then no one can be *a whole* by himself. Of a great whole all are parts. This is a doctrine whose moral glory and practical significance we yet dimly conceive.

But do we not according to this doctrine lose our own freedom and individuality? No. To be *part* of a wide communion, including many in mutual love and joint devotion, is the true personal estate, spiritual blessedness, individual honor, of each one. Who conceives of true individuality and noble liberty as being remoteness from humanity and indifference to one's race? All evil, real shame, and misery arise, when any one sets up to be a whole of himself. To aim at any separate completeness, to expect to be made by my own proper and peculiar success, to find my pride in anything but bringing myself, all I have and am, a contribution to the general good, — this and nothing else is sin, woe, and perdition. This is Antichrist, "that should come," and Antichristian, as the beloved

Apostle says, not to love one another. If we love one another, we cannot get rid of one another, but shall all be parts of one body.

Here is the great line of *classification* of human beings, into those who do or do not commune with others. We talk of communicants and non-communicants. Ah! this is more than an outside formal matter, of observing a particular ordinance, blessed as the observance will be to every sincere partaker. One loaf eaten, one cup tasted by many persons, is natural language, signifying the persons to be parts of one body with one circulation. But if the persons that eat and drink are not such parts, loaf and cup are nothing. The true communicant is he who by any exercise or service of duty or religion is led to feel his kindred with mankind as the offspring of God; and the non-communicant, he who in his heart feels no kinship with them, — yea, non-communicant, though he drank the wine of the Supper every month, or, like a Roman or Romanizing bishop or priest, consumed the remnant and ate up all the bread left on the table. "Members of churches in regular standing," we say. But they alone are living members of the Church who are unselfishly consecrated to that cause, of the Head of the Church, which is the cause of humanity.

This rule involves our whole human disposition and conduct. Are we laying up *money* for ourselves, and saying, as we lay it up, Ah! this is mine, my own, and belongs to nobody else! I will use it for my own purposes, or pile it into a heap for men's wonder and envy, that I may have the notability of vast possessions. The treasure shall belong to me, and none beside me; for none beside, beg and whimper with supplications and subscription-papers as they may, have any claim. I will count it over every day, and say within myself, *My property!* as I hear the clink of every coin, or feel the feathery touch of every note of value. In this way I may prove myself not a part of others, not a lively stone in the temple of Heaven's praise, not a bough in the tree of life, not an organ or function of the immortal body, — but an exclusive, self-seeking whole of my own. Prosper as I may seem to for a time, the result will be disappointment, with ering, disease and death; as it is with the sundered limb, the cast-off branch, the mouldering block, that might have been hoisted bright and strong into the dedicated edifice.

Disconnected, we perish by the laws of Christianity, — Christianity in its essence old as the moral creation of God in the human soul! It does not signify where or in what matter we attempt to be the whole; it is the same illness and iniquity. To be a Christian is to share joy, fame, every excellent thing, peace and salvation, with others. The monopolist, who in trade would control the market; who in social intercourse would be the observed of all observers, and do all the talking, it being a misnomer to call his conceited and unlistening monologue conversation; who of the fruits of any enterprise or partnership would appropriate the lion's share; who is a tyrant at home, allowing, like ten thousand other despots, more than sit on thrones, really no will or freedom in the household, like Louis XIV., who said, "I am the state"; who bids young children hold their tongue, as though they were not part also, when they actually have some reasonable and respectful plea to make, so that like a little boy lately they must go and pray God to give better tempers to their parents as well as themselves; — such a character in every situation, not content to be a part, claiming to be the whole, is unchristian and against the communion that is meant by the Lord's Supper.

This is a universal truth of nature and spirit. In all God's works we see the beautiful concord and proportion of parts composing a whole. In the midnight blaze you cannot point to a material orb, in its motion and revolution, but has this for the song the poet says it sings. How useless the moon, but as a part of the system with the earth she rises in mild splendor to enlighten! How like a lamp, left burning wastefully in a vacant room, were the sun, burning uselessly, wastefully in his great chamber of space, fit only to be blown out, save for the planets he fertilizes and illumines!

This wisdom, of parts making the goodness of the whole, is not confined to senseless matter; for how beautifully the philosopher of all animated nature shows every creature, from the lowest to the highest, as part of a great vital plan of the Creator, reaching down through amazing periods, that stagger and affright the imagination, of hundreds of thousands of years, and over the width of the globe! In every bird that stretches its flashing wings and flies, fish that swims the sea, every beast that runs or browses on the ground, rock-bound or creeping thing, how his eye detects, and the chalk-pencil in his fingers, by a modifying touch on the lines turning one structure into another in his figures on the board, can exhibit the thoughtful scheme of one glorious existence, rejoicing in myriad happy parts, individually alive, indissolubly connected! Nay, wonder on wonder, of the unity of workmanship of *the One*, only one everlasting Author of all, that there is not a grain, a leaf, a stalk, or a seed of the vegetable kingdom, which does not enter into, and in part compose, the higher kingdom of sentient life! One river flowing, flowing on for ever from God, the fount!

If God in his intelligence and action is consistent and like himself, the harmony of all creation's music, then moral natures, all our souls, are parts of the whole spiritual society of life and progress on earth and in heaven. We are to do each his several sacred office, whatever to every one for the common welfare that may be. If we are properly parts of one another, and of all humanity, we have no right either to exclude others or take away ourselves. If the finger should take itself away, it would not be merely the removal of a finger, but an injury to the hand; and the removal of hand or eye, a harm to the whole body. So humanity for its perfection wants all its members.

Indeed, for what did Jesus, sublimest of moral natures yet brought to our knowledge, come on earth? To be a whole, all by himself? Nay, but, on his own word and showing, to minister, and to declare that the least human creature, the obscurest sufferer of the race, was his representative; and he would take any kindness done to such a one as received by himself, the Lord of glory! Can we then have anything to do with Him at all as independent wholes, seeking each his own honor, riches, culture, nay, even everlasting redemption? No, but by being built up one building on him who is but part of the same, though the chief part and corner-stone!

After a sort, doubtless, we are so apparently joined together. In an engraved plate, recently published, of St. Peter's, that most wonderful cathedral in the world, we are shown the vast structure, in one engraving as it is, and in another alongside of it, as the architect, Michel Angelo, but for obstructions preventing, would have had it. Magnificent as the actual temple undoubtedly is, yet in every dome and door, porch and pillar in his model, his idea shines unspeakably superior to the edifice as it stands. So the Church of Christ as it stands is of a poor pattern, compared to that idea and model he set and lived out. The dead stones of St. Peter's cannot move themselves about into better positions of grace or grandeur; but the living stones of the human building, God helping, can!

Marvellous architecture of souls, not alone

in any earthly, but the heavenly building too! For heaven is no solitary, selfish existence, of individuals seeking their own separate progress and glory. We scarce read of any of its inhabitants being ever alone. They are in sevens and twelves, hundreds of thousands and multitudes no man can number. They fly in a flock to announce Christ's birth; they descend in company to minister to him after his trial; they come in pairs to sit in his tomb. In all their rest or journeying, alighting here or ascending to glory, they are social creatures, and parts of a whole. May we be like them while alive below, so that we may be with them when we die from the flesh into a higher life!

CHAPTER XVII.

FORM.

In the preceding chapters, through a great variety of reasonings and illustrations, I have endeavored to recommend open communion in the Congregational body. I am aware how disagreeably the proposal of such a change may strike many minds. One need not travel beyond his own consciousness and immediate observation to learn that man, as an individual and a species, is wedded to his habits. It seems easier to alter a principle of human procedure than a usage. How greatly ours is a Church of custom, not of Christ!

I know, too, how many may think the doctrine I have maintained disparages forms in general, and that its practical operation will appear less in the exaltation than in the neglect of the particular ordinance I have so much discussed. But has the opening of any other instrumentality of religion had this effect of weakness and dishonor? Has the Bible been hurt in its power by being opened to the people and translated for every nation into its own tongue! Has the church building been desecrated by having its seclusions abolished, and its space so widely exposed to all willing from the street to enter?

All forms may doubtless, by individuals admitted to the privilege thereof, be abused. But that is no argument against their proper use, or presumption contrary to their continuance. The forms of business are employed to cover every species of mercantile fraud. Under written documents, that look fair, lurks deceit. Solemn oaths are the ambush of perjury. Bonds and promises, certificates of property, duly drawn, signed and sealed, and decoratively marked, in their embellished numerals sometimes have their true value fictitiously quadrupled by a trick of speculation and a stroke of the pen. What low words, what winkings of the eye, of first owners, to the cost of last purchasers, pervert the forms of business indeed! Shall therefore those forms be set aside? Commerce itself would be set aside with them!

There are forms of law. Cunning men and unscrupulous advocates may turn them to purposes of injustice between contending parties at the tribunals of human courts. But shall all regular procedure be omitted? Then the net through which some of the wicked slip, would be too loose to catch any iniquity. There are forms of society. Through them love and good-will may be honestly expressed. But mere pretences may convert the most courteous company into a band of masqueraders, wearing visors, not on their faces, but their souls. Yet, with no forms at all, how rude and unmannerly men and women might become! How grace and order would flee away, like offended angels out of paradise! How the young would grow up in untutored awkwardness and native shyness, the rough substance of their nature taking no shape or polish from the common sense or common humanity of the race! Informality may be carried too far. What is a form, but a way in which, through many trials, mankind have learned best to accomplish matters of vital concern! It is not the essence, but it is an instrument and vessel of intellect and spirit. It is in religion a bottle of sacred odor, that suffers not the precious emotion, attained after long labor and suffering, to be wasted or spilled. It is a casket holding the gems of history, a vial containing the tears of the saints, the conservator of old piety and everlasting truth.

But all this worth and dignity of forms only prove the propriety, not of restricting, but more broadly extending, and, by every improvement and wise modification, adapting them to the common good. If new wine may never be put into old bottles, may not old wine sometimes well, if cautiously, be put into new? Partaking the feast of which millions have partaken, offering the prayer which for centuries has risen into God's ear, will not lose its virtue for the sympathetic heart on account of circumstantial variations.

When, therefore, as though to confute all argument for the open administration of the Supper, we are challenged to specify any times when persons became members of the Church without form, we answer, that of course there has always been form. Everything that lives and acts on earth must have its form. But no parallel can be drawn between our principle of exclusive and partial communion and that of the Christian Church in general, far less that of the mind of Christ and the primitive practice of his disciples. The true Church stretches out her arms, as the Lord does his, for the human race. She would baptize, confirm, and feed all born within her borders. It is the most burning criticism against her truth and purity, that, when any modern Diogenes with his lantern searches for a man, he is often as likely to go outside as inside her barriers of form, and, as not a few will say, sometimes more apt so to find the object of his pursuit.

I know much of this complaint against church-members may be but the jealous hypercriticism of coarse and unbelieving minds. So far as communicants have been personally known to me, I feel bound to testify to their general conformity to the professions they make, and the carping of such as set up to be better than the godly themselves, reminds one of Dr. Mason's reply to the sceptic denouncing some Christians for their misconduct,— Would such an uproar be made about the misbehavior of infidels?

Nevertheless, the level of the Church is far nearer than it should be to the level of the world. In ecclesiastical ordinances, as in other earthly things, men are sorely tempted to commit their great sin of converting the means into the end. A man seeks property wherewith to satisfy his worldly wants. But soon he seeks it for itself; and the great bulletin that now reports the whole planet at every man's door, lately told us of a rich miser perishing of starvation, because he could not spare enough from his hoard for his food. We obtain clothing to protect the body. But how often the dress itself becomes the object, and the person an appendage to the robe, instead of the robe an appendage to the person. How inordinate vanity displays, or affected modesty conceals, the human frame! How the health is sacrificed to the fashion of the garment, instead of promoted by it! How the style of some far-off imperial or queenly costume overcomes the simplicity of republican independence! Paris and London show their power over women and men in the back settlements, the wild woods, the newest parlors and meeting-houses of America, and extravagant outlay for stuffs and jewels helps bring on the financial disaster by which our civilization is well-nigh overwhelmed! The purpose of what we eat is to sustain the physical organization. But many, in their excess, make the meat more than life, and not the sexton in the churchyard, but they at their tables, dig their own graves. A good name is a means of right influence. But the name itself, in the shape of personal aggrandizement, political power, sectarian sway, and social repute, is by what numbers sought!

So we come to church to praise God and commune with Christ. But with what multitudes the temple becomes more than the deity! Graven images and figures of wood and stone were doubtless at first but religious means. The most ignorant African idolaters, when reproached for their superstitions, say, as decidedly as do the Romanists of their material signs, it is not the statue, picture, or animal that they worship, but only the incomprehensible Power. Yet how soon the means become the end, and how wise therefore the old Mosaic command against any likeness of divinity! But, if we stop in our more refined ceremonial, are not we idolaters too? It is idolatry, we may say, to substitute the Mediator for the Supreme One in our worship. It is grosser idolatry to adore the virgin mother of Jesus as the mother of God, and to call, as once he was called, even the brother of Jesus according to the flesh the brother of God. The still descending steps that lead to worship of the saints, whose names should be but our starry ladder into the heavens, are idolatrous to the very scandal of every pious thought. Yet, if we put any part of our ritual, even the Lord's Supper, for the end instead of the means, how undeniably of an idol-loving heart are we ourselves! If Jesus Christ had been told, the time would come when his figures of speech, respecting his own body and blood, would be regarded more than his loftiest declarations of truth and most solemn precepts of duty, and his literal words more esteemed than his deepest thoughts, what would he have said, but that, in his knowledge of human nature and prophetic foresight of events, he was doing all he could to prevent so lamentable a result! Yet how many are so wedded to precise modes of worship, that a spontaneous petition, born of the soul's commerce with God and baptized with tears, seems to them, as indeed they coolly declare it, *no service at all!*

Jesus himself truly did all, everything in his power to break up religious routine. When he plucked the corn on the Sabbath day, he meant to pluck up superstition by the roots. Yet even now behold the Church dying of ceremony! Zion, at her ease, is a captive to the world. What uniform authority can however be brought for the present invariableness of a single usage? The Manichæans, never using wine, celebrated the Eucharist without it, and I believe they have some modern imitators in that respect. Christ himself, instituting the Supper, showed how little of a formalist he was, in anticipating the Jewish Passover by one day. In the lower creatures the vital system is spread upon the outside, but in the nobler ones hid at the centre. So, according to the degree in which it is superficial or internal, is the dignity of our religion. *Form* we must have: for though the solitary soul may be religious without visible sign, a number of persons must meet upon some terms. The incomparable spirituality of Jesus accepted and appointed ordinances; and in exercises of social religion, for the new-born or the just expiring, who has not shared amid domestic scenes too incalculably precious ever to be forgotten? The Church, in foreign towns, sometimes making the avenue of her porch the very pathway of men to their business, must do something thus to sanctify the exchange and market. While nature's emblems last, and the sun speaks of God's countenance, the driven snow of his purity, and the morning dew of his influence; so long shall the Christian symbols endure, and not arbitrary signs of words alone, but language of form and action, speak to the human soul.

I suppose there is no such thing as a purely private experience in the world; and therefore, perhaps, take no unwarranted liberty in telling a true story, that thousands might match from their own lives. I stood, not long since, in a wilderness of rocks, lying a little inland from one of the deep indentations of our Atlantic shore. For miles around me stretched the brown waste, bare of almost everything but a multitude no man could number, in various size and shape, of those gray boulders, to account for whose form, nature, and position — whether piles of floating ice were the ships to carry them on primeval floods, or sliding glaciers bore them down from inconceivably ancient, now sunken mountains, or torrents washed smooth the fragments and angles that earthquakes and lightnings broke off — is the puzzle and controversy of our science. To the thoughtful eye their forms of antiquity were more venerable than sphinxes or pyramids, and the natural inscriptions of their history or their faces, could we read them, would be more interesting than all that has been deciphered on Egyptian obelisks or Herculanean walls. They seemed pieces left of the material of which God made the frame of the world. Bits they were of the mighty bones of Nature thrown away, or the heaps of chips and shavings which fell from the marvellous tools of the first workmanship ever set up amid the void of chaos in the space of old night. They took stronger hold of the mind's wonder than do any familiar and finished shapes of hill and vale. Lying couchant on the ground, they looked almost like monsters of the antique world, stiffened into stone, that might as in a moment leap forth into life again. The wildest birds, that usually seek the highest tree-tops, lighted in huge companies on the summits, scattered along the uneven and billowy soil, — while on either hand from afar shone the ring of the blue sea which had ebbed and flowed from the dawn of creation.

Altar sublime of the Creator's glory was that at which I stood. But why did the heart, in its unsatisfied longing, revert to a shrine infinitely smaller, of uncomely brick and wood? Because it stands for the moving of God's love to his human children, whom he called into being incalculable ages after he wrought the tough substances of the globe. Because its walls and tower, though plain, are monuments of facts more directly and tenderly related to the benefit of man, than the first hewing and shaping of the world for enormous growths of vegetable and animal life. Because they tell of the incarnation of Deity in our own nature, beside and above his embodiment and tabernacle in senseless dust. Because they express tidings of a spiritual world more clearly than do any of the things materially made. Because they speak to the sinner of a hope, which lawful and unpardoning nature never inspired, and of a heaven that earth's stairway leads up to only through dimness and doubt. Because, for all these reasons, in dedicated courts we can render social worship richer, more honorable to God and comforting to the soul, than ever rose out of his first temples, be they of the forest or the clay.

If God has made a disclosure of himself and of his abode, for our dwelling too after we leave this mortal tent, let there be an observance by the children to whom he has made it, of sufficient form to recognize and appropriate his mercy. I have seen a flock of birds, as it flew by the edge of the sepulchral sea, shot at by a gunner from the rocks. But as one of their number fell into the foaming wave, the rest kept on heedless of its solitary fate. If so a human being does not fall, if his fellows stop to lift and mourn and bury him, and follow some deathless part to a sunnier clime than is sought by the emigrant fowls of the air, how largely is this sentiment due to the religion of Jesus Christ! How, then, together should we celebrate that religion, but by so much of observance as shall make it most alive to his united disciples?

CHAPTER XVIII.

PERSON.

In any such discussion as I have been pursuing, we must consider, of course, not alone the method of unfolding religion as a general sentiment in the human breast, but also of establishing the generations in a properly Christian faith. Now Christianity is no abstraction of sentiment or belief. What is peculiar to it, and essential in it, is the person of its author. Christ himself, not simply the historic Christ, once in a human body, but the surviving, ever-living Redeemer, is the heart and soul and endless preservation of his Gospel. Here is the hold on mankind of the Supper, that it is a rite whose tendency is to bring them into a nearer personal relation with the Son of God. What is the style in which he addresses us? "Come unto me, all ye that labor and are heavy laden, and I will give you rest. Take my yoke upon you, and learn of me: for I am meek and lowly in heart; and ye shall find rest unto your souls. For my yoke is easy, and my burden is light." What must strike every attentive reader is the exceedingly *personal* character of such language, — the words *I*, *my*, and *me*, recurring in it so often, expressing no egotism, but only humility and humanity to the tired, overtasked children of men; yet still, as the solace, Jesus offers to those beat out with their burdens no distinct idea or minute disclosure of his views respecting their present trouble or revelation of things to come, only himself.

But this Christian method has, in addition to the warrant of Scripture, the confirmation of nature. When we are worn out and distressed in any way, whither do we turn for relief? To such generalities of argument as we can bring from reason or memory to our aid, or to SOMEBODY, some friend, relative, trusted counsellor and guide, wise, good, affectionate, to minister to the mind dejected or diseased? We

"Fly like a bird of the air,
In search of a home and a rest;
A balm for the sickness of care,
A bliss for a bosom unblest."

O to hear the voice, to take the hand, to sit by the side, and have the personal assurance, of one in whom we confide! How many, with hopes blasted, and goods scattered in recent whirlwinds of adversity, for such help received can respond to this! If such a one, in such a case relied upon, be absent, out of our reach, what is the sad and bitter exclamation, but, O, if my companion, partner, brother, sister, were only with me now, and I could lean my aching head on his bosom, and feel his gentle hand pouring balm into my bleeding wounds, how were I blessed and soothed! So exclaimed the sisters to Jesus: "If thou hadst been here, our brother had not died!" So cried the disciples: "Lord, to whom shall we go? Thou hast the words of eternal life!"

What, therefore, some doubters object to the Christian faith, — namely, that it is so personal, that, instead of reasons, considerations, for the pure intellect, a person, sent to deliver, fills in it so much space,—by the testimony of human nature as well as the appointment of Heaven, is not its defect, but its power and glory; for it has been well said, though we may believe propositions, only in persons can we have faith.

But, admitting this in the actual personal ministry of Christ eighteen and a half centuries ago, when his benignant form and voice, look and manner, drew the discouraged and afflicted, sick men and women and weeping mourners, from Judæa and beyond Jordan to his side, it may yet be inquired, how can he, now indeed absent and invisible so long, be to us a person at all, far more a personal comforter in our weakness and grief? I answer, his concealment from our senses certainly does not destroy his personality. It does not destroy or cancel the comfort of any one's. The support we derive from mortal persons does not depend altogether upon having them in sight, or in the room. If we have ever come to know and love their personality, it is an inextinguishable power, strong to uplift.

If we are sure of their sympathy, it reaches from their houses over all smoke and noise and street confusion to our own, or follows us, like a guide and companion, in our farthest steps. If they have ever said, or in their countenance expressed, anything of genuine fellow-feeling for our infirmities and sufferings, then, without sound or look, it flies to our succor in every hour of our sore extremity and want. Yea, testifieth the heart that knoweth, when mountains rise, and oceans roll between us and them, their gracious images come, not by help of mail or telegraph, but supernatural visiting; their faces shine how wondrously, in the darkened chambers of our solitary bosoms; not general calculations and judgments sustain and carry us through our trials, but their spirits dear to us troop through the air to people our loneliness, and revive our despondency, or their undoubted regard mixes sweetness with the tears we shed, and makes us, by God's grace, content still to live. Nay, down from the heavenly places descends that cloud of witnesses which the Apostle celebrates, for spectators to cheer us in the panting, dusty race of life: and it is persons, persons always, in the flesh or immortalized, and not our own independent reasonings, that we lean upon in the tug of calamity at our wasted strength.

No wolf shall come to our door, no despair sit in our souls, while any most fading likeness of friends hangs on our wall, or from within irradiates our path, or from their vanishing forms beams down upon our hope. Not ideas alone affect, but persons; — they indeed can warm or freeze, attract or repel, bless or curse, ruin or save! We think we live in a world of matter, or in a world of thought. It is partiality and mistake. We live in a world of persons. We need only call to mind birth-places and homes, our closest connections in life, our refuges from the world's coldness, enmity, and misrepresentation, and our soothings in pain, peril, and sickness, to know this. In respect to that fashion of our philosophy, to say truth is everything and persons are nothing, the individual, the living man of no account, I ask, What is truth but the relation of persons to one another, and of a personal God and Father to his children? For what was the world made, and home built in heaven above? For absolute ends of unconscious essence? Never, but for persons alone!

Therefore, when Jesus appears, the great Person, to his titles of glory so many and so high let me add this, of the greatest person "that e'er wore flesh about him" to be touched and tempted like ourselves, on purpose to understand our woe, and have fellowship with every feeling of exposure in the human breast, and, through miracles of strength, and loftier marvels of love and purity, to declare his office of communion and encouragement, not for a few transient acquaintances, but to heal the miseries of the human race, there is nothing of experience or principle to reject, but only to welcome him, who alone has taught us what it fully is to be a person, a conscious existence from the inspiration of God, "the Desire" indeed, as he is called, "of all nations," and Physician of maladies deeper than the perishable frame.

A mere herald with messages from on high, — as I have heard him called, — a bringer of moral precepts, a foreteller of future facts in another state, the whole significance of his being and advent exhausted in his literal communications? Nay, this, so far from being religion, is not the fact in influence of any kind, however earthly and low. It is not so with any common actor on the historic stage. Not what the heroes of this world have done to alter the face of the earth and shift the course of events, not what new announcements for human welfare from the realm of invention they have brought, but what they themselves, the persons, have been, moves our deepest concern. Witness the unquenchable and everlasting interest in every flower of humanity, distinguished individual of our race, which makes of "all history only biography"! Therefore upon canvas or into enduring marble their heads are thrown, that successive generations may possess them in their fellow-creatures' never-weary gaze. Newton, Howard, Washington, — for what do they stand but for truth, benevolence, and patriotism?

To take from the host of social, political, and scientific benefactors of mankind a single recent case, — when the brave adventurer goes, with sacrifice of comfort, surrender of health, and offer of life, to make, if possible, the dreary Arctic Sea plain and safe to following navigators, — to the absorbed reader of his thrilling narrative, not what Kane discovered of icebergs or circumpolar currents on that dreadful coast, wondrous as those discoveries were, and affect human knowledge or future explorations as they may, but what in nobility of soul, Christian disinterestedness, and trust in the All-Fatherly God, Kane was, quivers on the heart-strings and moistens the beaming lids.

But that Person which has made other persons noble and good from the baptism of fire of its own holy sublimity and love; which walked in Jerusalem only to fill the world with its presence; which heaven is not big enough to hold, for it reaches yet into the earth; which is ever ready to enter into every wretched heart, hearing and opening to its knock, since the swollen eyes of Mary and Martha were dried before it, — O ye that still come at its old but never obsolete invitation, what shall I say of *that* person, — yea, of THAT?

What, but to repeat its gracious summons, "Come unto me!" For the overborne and spent among mortals he is the Person. There is none such as he. I will not dispute that various other persons and conspicuous personages in the world's history may be followed by different men and classes according to their tastes and fancied necessities, if to the great Christian allegiance they cannot be won; — or if, as sometimes, though with what ignorance, they say they are too young or too happy to be religious. But we at least, who have been weary and heavy laden, will cling to this Son of God. They whose chief admiration is the bold and martial conqueror, — subduing tribes and territories to his sway, — may enshrine and idolize the Napoleons and Cæsars in their imagination, and think it a grand thing to imitate them on the little scale of a state or town, an office or hearth-stone. They whose mind kindles supremely at the beauty of art, may above all envy and copy the great masters in color and stone, in material structures or written words. They who adore nature and natural knowledge may set human science above the model of a perfect life in Him above all beside moral Ruler, and in the highest of arts Master indeed. They who are "happy now," because not a string on the fine instrument of their health and self-indulgence, like some performer's at the fine concert, has cracked from its holdings, may make, not purity, but pleasure their god. But they who in this world have felt what it is to be burdened with disappointment, bereavement, poverty, and disease, will come to Him who can give them rest.

In the courts of law or at the bar of public opinion the humblest persons are admitted to testify to facts coming within the sphere of their observation; and their testimony, if honest, is by eloquent advocates and judges on their seats admitted as authority in the case. There are facts falling so often under notice we can scarce be mistaken in their character, or deemed quite unqualified for their report. That this unparalleled Person, whom we call Jesus Christ, reverently introduced at the bedside of the sick; that his name, — what a spell it has hung alike over cradle and grave of mankind! — only his name in a prayer falling on the ear of the dying; that the voice of his word, reaching the soul of those sobbing over the clay which so lately was child, brother, parent, friend, and now is like any other clod, — affords peace unspeakable for sinking and doubt and indescribable loss, there are ten thousand witnesses.

Our whole humanity indeed does that divine Person address. The conqueror may come to him who has gained a mightier victory over death; the statesman, to him who has established a kingdom beyond his policy; the artist, the workman in any material, to him whose life has laid out stints challenging and foiling all tools, pen, or pencil; and young and gay, pleased and allured as they are, may come to be more refreshed and blessed. But the weary and burdened with age, misfortune, and suffering, — O, because of their inexpressible need is *his* particular call! Do any, not knowing yet, perchance, what it is to be worn out or wretched, say they do not belong to this class? They are not old, they are not diseased, they are not disappointed, they are not bereaved, they are not (do they know that?) on the brink of the grave! But upon whom will the burden and weariness not, if already they have not, come? God only knows how heavy and sharp, in our separation, our destitution, our pain or expiring sigh, the load will press. On the shoulder that bore the cross, he allows us to lean. Is it then one portion and order, or the whole species, all of us, as human creatures, his terms embrace?

No illusion or ecstasy can carry us beyond this foundation of Christ's claim. We are persons. A person greater than we must save us. The person over all is God; but the greatest personality incarnate in our nature for our rescue is Christ. So long as we are living persons, too, talk not of transports of genius or love as contradicting this doctrine! They only confirm it. The imagination whose wings uplift, and the love whose warmth melts my soul, are my imagination and love. Like the microscopic dot of life, which makes the whole mass it appears in its food, I am the centre of the circle of my faculties, and nothing less than the universe is that on which

I feed. Beyond all else is our interest in persons. Witness two continents search the Pole for one missing crew! This living monad in us of indissoluble unity is our only hope. When present accesses to it through the fleshly organization close in death, this asks for other channels. It feels indestructible. When it knows itself, it knows its immortality. It is the self the prodigal must come to, before he can go to his Father. In Jesus alone this personal glory was complete. In him, of all others, the personality of a humanly divine nature has come of age. He, in truth, beauty, wisdom, and goodness, is what a person should be. Such a person falls under no measure of space or time, but takes hold of infinity and eternity. Such an one, exceeding our attainment and criticism, and mighty to fashion us above ourselves, in his Supper we signify that he is. But who, desiring to be at all moulded by his hand, shall not freely join in the sign?

CHAPTER XIX.

PLACE.

It is to a certain extent a surprise, if not an offence, in our particular denominational latitude of the Church, that the Lord's Supper should be taken into the same circle with the other services of his religion. But in so associating it we only follow his own manner. How was it at first? How did he do himself? He discoursed, he prayed, he sang, — would his song had been recorded for us! — as well as ate and drank, with his disciples. He did all these things at the same time together with them, as much as we converse while eating and drinking in company at our own tables. He did not set one of these services apart from or above another. He did not admit one of his disciples to one of them, and exclude him from any other. He made no one of these services a test, profession, or privilege, more than any other. He himself was not less holy or gentle or good in one of them than in another. Out of honor for him, respect for his example, and love to his flock, we shall unite what he united. If we will follow Christ's example, our preaching and prayer and praise should not, on the day of communion, be separated from his table. Doctrine, precept, devotion, and ritual should be in harmony. Is one part of the building more dedicated than another? Font and board, pulpit and pew, choir and speaker and hearer, should be joined in one body, however called, Church or Congregation.

All the Lord's sayings and doings belong together. He specifies or allows in them no such separation into more or less sacred, marked and professional, as is often made. They make the unity he implores for his followers. It is profanation to pick and choose and part them.

This local and circumstantial unity, if I may call it so, composes the picture of that Jerusalem where the incidents mostly transpired, and causes it to be so complete and congruous to our mind. The model of the Holy City, as we know, has been sculptured, painted, lithographed, engraved, and carried round for exhibition in panoramas through the world. But what is its world-wide charm? From what ancient national glory of a whole Hebrew race does it draw so much interest as from the harmonious history of that wonderful person in whom God and man met in unison? Behold in the mind's eye this far-off place! The area of the temple where he disputed with the doctors and worshipped the Father; the roads he walked to Bethany and Siloam, Samaria and Galilee, faintly indicated on maps; the valley of Jehoshaphat into which he descended; the brook Kedron he crossed; the garden of agony, where his sweat seemed to mingle with his blood; the hill, on one side, of his midnight supplications, and on the other of his noonday crucifixion; the sepulchre where he was buried, and the spot whence it is thought he rose; with some little indefinable points the eye wanders after to find if possible,—the judgment-hall of Pilate or the upper chamber of the feast; — over all these he casts the equal and invariable dignity of his life and presence. For what reason indeed is it that such things as these, and no wars or rumors of wars there, are the salvation to an earthly immortality of glory of that old Jewish capital, keeping it in the world's gaze and centre for ever? Not when or by whom Jerusalem was founded or taken, overthrown or rebuilt, but the life and death of one singular personage, more than of millions beside, hallow and endear its streets with the various circumstances of his career. These features, on the holy canvas hung before our imagination, all belong together. We cannot expunge one of them, and not destroy the keeping of the whole; and we cannot insulate Christ's table in particular from his general religion without a blot, which he never made.

Place, then, as well as reason and symbol, and all the other considerations I have enumerated, is an argument for the universal fellowship in every respect of the members of his school. The Egyptians swathed some little figure of royal flesh for centuries of ghastly honor; he, by the uniform grandeur his deportment shed over it, embalmed a whole metropolis for living and everlasting fame. It is Jerusalem verily as he thus made it, and not a certain town, with an estimated population, at a fixed era, flourishing in the geography of the planet, that we care for. Long ages before his birth were its walls reared, synagogues set up, and gates opened. Generations after he vanished, the Romans razed it to the ground, permitting but three of its towers to stand. But, account for it as sceptic or believer may, all the hosts, earlier or later, that trampled about it, left no such print in the soil as those feet of one person, which, under the weight of the cross, trod the *via dolorosa*, the painful way to Golgotha, place of a skull, of ashes and death, but centre and source of spiritual life to all succeeding generations.

Jerusalem! it is no material ground, no mechanical structure, but a creation of power by Christ's sympathy for all people and lands. Not one or another, but every act and word alike of his distinguishes and consecrates its space. Jerusalem! it has no mere earthly latitude and longitude. It is situate in the mind! It is part of the moral territory of every pious heart. It is annexed to every Christian country. It is within the precincts of every most remote church on the face of the globe. It is lifted into heaven and called New Jerusalem there, built of jasper and sapphire and pearl and amethyst, precious metal and precious stones, to signify a beauty to the soul of which all terrestrial treasure is but the glimmer and shade.

Marvellous and incomparable testimony of Christ's, beyond any human power, that he has woven the annals of the place over which he wept, as so broad a band, into the web of universal history, and, as towns on new continents are called after those on old ones, has carried up into the sky its name, therewith to baptize the eternal city of the Great King; so as to make in these last times myriads of loving enthusiasts in every zone sing,

"Jerusalem, my happy home!"

and give the title on earth of that New Jerusalem to perhaps the most spiritual and imaginative of all religious sects! "Jerusalem

Delivered" is the title of the great Italian poem, written to celebrate the feats of the Crusaders, when all Europe cast itself on Asia to rescue the Saviour's tomb. But Jerusalem was delivered, and, beyond all the decays and corruptions of time, is preserved to the lively concern of the human family's latest descendants, for whatever is most distinctive in its story, by the events of the marvellous biography of him whom his Evangelists knew not whether to call Son of God or Son of Man. So was he, and so he styled himself, both, and so, truly considered, both are for ever one and the same.

Place, then, I say, the argument of history, record, locality, in the indissoluble unity which his character gave it, I present as a persuasive for our unity. Is one of us more than another interested in the local circumstances that embodied his spirit and life? Does a portion of the Christian community respond to the feeling those circumstances move, and the rest not? Would the heart in some of our bosoms thrill at actual sight of the ground in Judæa where he journeyed and suffered, and, in other of our breasts, be indifferent and cold! God forbid! But if it be so, God forbid that we should attempt, by any ecclesiastical judgment, to tell who would burn and who be lukewarm! Jesus, who could judge, did not classify and divide his disciples. Let not us! Judge or accurately divide we cannot. He was content if any emotion stirred their souls toward him where he was. Heaven touch us all, by every common exercise that may remind us where he was, and what he did and said and felt in our behalf! Therefore let our social commemoration of him, for the identity he carried through every passage of his life put on no point any schism in our fellowship or practice. In teaching, command, or emblem of his religion, let us be one, as he entreated and of his entreaty, that we might not violate it, provided that we should so distinctly know

This local argument becomes more convincing, when we consider the position of Christ's last Supper with his disciples in its future reference. His table was spread on the edge of the world. It stood between the seen and unseen states. Just beyond was the eternity into which he was about to step out of time. He says unto them, "I will not drink henceforth of this fruit of the vine, until that day when I drink it new with you in my Father's kingdom." There was a place then, another place over the flood which he was so soon to tempt, where he would assemble all believers in him,—irrespective of their diversities of nature and attainment, wise and ignorant, of capacity original or common, of temperament steadfast or variable, more cool or zealous in enterprise, if they only wanted to be with him,—for more blessed and lasting communion; even as loyal John and fickle Peter, doubting Thomas and matter-of-fact Matthew, with others whose individuality was not strong enough to show their faces clearly through the dim distance to our gaze, met around him in one circle which he did not break with any severe moral discriminations on earth. Ah! with our denominational tests and technicalities and creeds, we make heaven too small, and make it undesirable,—a place not really attractive, but a habitation of cliques and parties, into which no generous and humane soul wishes to go! So Jesus made it not for his followers. All now who are sincerely associated to worship God in the name of his Son, as much as they, are believers. We, like them, may be more or less unworthy; but the fact of our Christian association is the pledge of our faith, unless we be pretenders and hypocrites in the very terms of our union.

From a sense of unfitness, which the Lord regards as no disqualification, do we hesitate to partake the memorials of his regard here? But shall we not wish to partake those other predicted memorials there? Those dear to us as our own life, whose now cold hands and sealed lips perhaps once partook these emblems, or peradventure declined them because they were not offered to all, — do we doubt their participation in every gracious token of fellowship in that "general assembly and church of the first-born," where "one star differeth from another star in glory," yet none cordially aspiring are excluded from the great sphere of love and joy? Could they speak to us, — nay, could we hear their call, — would it not sound in our bosom louder than the ring-ing of a church-bell, exhorting us, when every symbol of grace to the honest seeker is offered, not to refuse? Once only, in a life strewn with deaths and lined with graves, as if spent in a churchyard, have I attended a funeral where not a drop of kindred blood was present to mourn. The air, as I breathed it, and sunshine, as I looked on it, were melancholy round the coffined clay. But will not the affections that have waited round and glorified the ashes of our beloved, claim in heaven the fellowship of their souls?

Let us have the fellowship with them and with one another now below! Let the scenes of Christ's divine appearance in humanity win us to him and reconcile us among ourselves. O, could any earthly relics of him be found, how eagerly would they be gathered up, and how superstitiously cherished! Those thorns of his brow would be chased every one in gold; every grain of the wood and rough tree of his cross set in diamond; every thread of his mock-purple robe — indeed most kingly ever worn, mock as it was — knit in bracelets of pearl; every particle of the rock sepulchre prized above all the rare stones and gems ot the East; and for his bones, — O, for his bones, could they be brought to light, how crowns would be bartered and princes dispute! Cannot what is spiritual of him be reckoned at a rate as high as the material would be? Lo! of the material, we have nothing, not a jot. If we had it, its adoration were but our idolatry. Of the spiritual we have all; and, verily, it should link us to him and to one another!

CHAPTER XX.

ORGANIZATION.

I HAVE been considering the Church, not as an invisible fraternity of faith and charity, but as a visible, working brotherhood, in order to give full force to the objection, which may now be made, that by opening its communion we lose its organization. To this objection I reply, that it puts for the cause an effect. Eating the Supper together does not organize the body, but is something the organized body does. Members of the Church may sit at the table; but sitting at the table does not make them members. The Supper implies, not constitutes, membership. Their membership is their common trust and love for their Lord; and these principles, not any forms, are the true organizing power. Those brought into unison by these principles are organized, though they decline to partake of the feast;

as the Quakers are organized while they sit and silently wait for the moving of the Spirit.

Romish writers dwell much on the true "Notes" of the Church. A solemn and affectionate observance of the ordinances of the Church is doubtless one of these Notes. The ordinances are means no doubt indispensable to the mass of men, morally infirm as they are, prepossessed by the senses, wedded to the world, and wanting something visible and striking with holy associations to win them from what is earthly and profane. But how radical the mistake of putting any superficial demonstrations above the more authentic spiritual signs! I have seen a government vessel on the coast take soundings of the waters, and re-measure the lines of the shore. But if she had regarded only the surface, and cared nothing for the depth, she would have committed for the seaman only the blunder of those formalists who have not penetrated the depths of the spirit, yet think themselves of Christ's Body, when they are but intruders into his company, and hangers-on to his train.

No measurement, indeed, is better than a false one; for men are less likely to be destroyed in the conscious ignorance that makes them cautious in feeling their way, than by the conceit of knowledge that makes them rush on, bold and foolhardy. For the Church itself it is less safe to rely on its external agencies than on its internal powers. Does not the steam-ship go both more swift and secure than the sailing vessel? Availing herself of inward forces, from the breakers' edge she steers back into the teeth of the storm, and wins the open sea, when oar and canvas, rudder and pilot, cannot save the full-rigged barque, with all the boast of her snowy canvas, from wreck. So, valuable as outward impulses are in their place for those feebly beginning to navigate the sea of life, the central motives of love and righteousness save the Church and the human soul from disaster and death, when wholly in vain may be the ceremonies, of which so many make but a scarcely better substitute than the old Jewish legalities themselves. Precious instrumentalities indeed are Christian ordinances; but the mistake of holding them for the topmost or in any way essential part of the Christian religion, will expose itself at a moment's thought. If we can conceive of part of that religion as falling away, would it not be the ordinances sooner than the doctrine, far sooner than the spirit and the law? If we would excuse a man from any part of the religion, surely it would not be the precepts, but the rites. Nay, can we honestly fetch any moral blame of our own, or condemnation from the mouth of Christ, against a person, merely for his omission of those rites? Those rites, I believe, have a long date of existence yet before them, appealing as they do, through the heart and imagination, to the soul; but none can think the eternity of principles is theirs. Leaning upon mere rites for our redemption is but a poorer sort of that morality, and a meaner kind of those works of the law, which the Apostle decries as impotent for our rescue.

I know the real virtues of the soul are often theologically despised, in comparison with obscure processes and mysterious manipulations. But I know, too, the heart of the world exclaims, Would that, of the truth, justice, faithfulness, and of all those things disparaged by bigots and sectarians under the title of *mere amiable affections*, there were more! Then the world were safer to live in than it is. Then there were more integrity in business, innocence in pleasure, candor in society, peace in families, and purity in private life. Ordinances by themselves, as they are too often observed, are but a cold moon of seeming purity, rising after the orb of day has set, losing the warmth of the beam they reflect; cordial dispositions of love are the sun quickening all nature into life.

By ecclesiastical facts, as well as spiritual principles, this position is confirmed. Where formalists are met together, what a chill steals through the building, as in a room where the fire declines! Whole Gospels and Epistles might be brought in proof that, however forms in their place may and do serve us, Christianity was never meant for a formal religion. The soul of inspiration knew our human life to be an ocean, and therefore it gave us a system, not of hard fixture like a house on its unmoving foundations, but rather like a boat, which may well be made in great pictures a sacred symbol, adapting itself to the throbbing heart of humanity, stooping lowly to conquer, yet riding on the crest of the waves. The Gospel is a light for us. It is a breath upon us. It is a well within us. Something fresh, shining, flowing and reviving, is its nature.

Aiming to be perfectly just, setting my heart on sincerity and truth in describing it, I must say the proportion of form to substance in it is very small. It uses no more machinery than is necessary, — only enough to get along with, — just as, in an engine, the fewer the rods and levers consistently with the transmission of power, the less the friction and mightier the result. Therefore Christianity has lived, survived all changes, and surmounted all opposition. Had it been a mere scheme of dogma or ritual, it would have been swept away, dissolved, and long ages since in its grave. There would have been nothing of it left, more than of the ark upon Ararat, if it had been built of outward material, like the ark of wood. But, contrariwise, how broad it is, and free and spiritual! It does not limit the Divine impulse to its own written pages, but offers it to "every man that cometh into the world." It empowers every true child of God, not only to repeat a literal text, committed to memory, but to speak in his Father's name. Many are they that speak conventionally from the world, and never in the name of God. But so Christians may speak. Why should not every one, feeling drawn by the Father to his Son, partake his Supper without other condition? By any terms or exclusiveness of our own to send away those thus drawn, is the arch heresy of tearing the body of Christ.

This free and vital observance alone is worthy; for here is the distinction between the child and the slave, that the latter can but recite the phrase, or do with mechanical exactness the thing, being influenced and directed only from without, from man and the world; but the former acts and utters from within, from the Infinite Mind. In fellowship with Christ, the dear Son, he takes thoughts and monitions from the Supreme at first hand. The Holy Spirit does not quote. It alone never refers. It pronounces with direct truth and authority through the breast it visits. This is the doctrine of holiness, an internal principle alone. No thing is holy, only feeling and thought are such. The sea is not itself holy. It can be no more than an image of the holiness of those who are the salt of the earth. The air is not pure; but only the pure in heart. No ceremonial is holy beyond the purpose of those who administer or receive it. Not to create a friend's love, or to learn it, but to strengthen it, do we desire and use tokens. So is it with the love of God.

Those in this spiritual state in any religious society will be united and organized indeed! There need be no fear about their harmony, co-operation, or efficiency. They may be owners of pews; but they will not be associated upon a secular basis. Their proprietorship will be but an incident, not the essence. Their pews will be opened to friend or stranger, rich or poor, bond or free; and to represent the pew-system, thus administered for Christian purposes, as implying that the whole foundation of the institution wherein it prevails is pecuniary and selfish, inflicts, however undesignedly, upon millions of men a wrong as great as can be in any untruth. The members of the Lord's Body may or may not be legal possessors of ground or building they occupy. Their names may or may not be recorded in a book; but no inscription or omission of a name will constitute, and no want of oral or verbal pledge vacate, their organization. It may be convenient for them, as a corporation, to be known to the law; but no law of the land, only the higher law of God, operating through the spirit of Christ, will be their bond.

The spiritual life doubtless requires circumstantial aids in addition to secret refreshments; and all means that have in them any furtherance are valuable in precise proportion to the worth of the end, just as is the bread that sustains life, the medicine that cures disease, or the staff that stands between us and danger. But no ministrations can create life, or preserve it after the constitutional vitality from body or mind is gone. I admit the practical difficulties. Nothing is harder to determine than the kind and amount of ecclesiastical organization in any given circumstances best suited to transmit the Divine Spirit. If we attempt anywise to tie up the wonderful and holy element, it drops out. If we seek not by any social band to secure it, we may fail to get or touch it at all. But, according as we see the relation of the means to the end, we shall be less disposed to hold our modes to any hard shape, which Christ does not enjoin, and allow the utmost flexibility and variety. We shall not quarrel with diversity, and stickle for uniformity in the mode of any observance, as many portions of the Church so absurdly do. How irrational and unwise this formal rigor would be in everything else! Would the manners of men and nations be more beautiful, if, instead of the range of liberty they take, they were all run in the same iron mould? The essence is not in any matter sacrificed with the shape. Commerce, with its present marvellous facilities, is at bottom the identical thing it was, when —

instead of gold and silver, and notes and bonds — an ox or a skin, a bushel of wheat, Spartan iron, or a cowry-shell, as still in Africa, was its token. Society arises from the same fundamental sentiments as with the tribes whose caravans, moving different ways, exchanged greetings in the desert; for one human heart beats in city-blocks and amid whirling sands. So the principles of our faith change not, widely variant with latitudes and centuries as may be their style; for the style is not the thing, any more than the straw is the current, or the sea-mark the sea. Vanes of a thousand fashions on our steeples may show one direction of the wind; and many diverse practices and customs without contradiction indicate the course of the same Spirit. These practices and customs will pass or change. Many a Jericho even now is tumbling down. Truly there is trouble in every camp. We may well be charitable to manifold modes, if it be true, as a great Methodist lately told me, that no creed or church-organization in the world can defend itself, or put a bad man where he belongs, or claim God's acceptance. Have we not departed, all of us, not only from the primitive, but from the best days of the later Church, whenever we confound substance and show in religion? Of course there must be signals of Christian faith and feeling. I only contend, they should be freely open for the education and reception of the whole body, instead of being used as a line of judgment to divide the one body visibly in two parts rising over against and confronting one another. The old Latin fathers sharply distinguished between realities and forms, though the former have too much degenerated into the latter in the Transalpine Church.

This confusion of reality with form is, however, working mischief how far beyond the borders of Rome! The census of New England and New York proves but an annual addition of one or two members for every particular local church, in this wide domain of the unsurpassed and concentrated intelligence of Christendom, — an unpromising ratio surely of increase, when we consider how death is ever at work, not forbearing to intrude into every enclosure with the law of his dealing upon life. Death, bodily death, will be the devourer of spiritual life on earth very soon, at this rate. But let us resist and raise bars to his reign. Let us train childhood into the Church, and by the law of life so counter-charm that of death. Let not our offspring grow up Pagan. Admission to the Jewish synagogue, except for adult proselytes, was a matter of hereditary right, and the circumcision of infants a domestic ceremony. Let baptism, the solemn dedication of the young, be with us no less common and familiar, as a door leading, by the path of growth and confirmation in Christian graces, to the Lord's Supper. Is the principle of training less in its moral and spiritual, than in its confessedly intellectual truth? Has God promised to give us grace and virtue unconditionally, more than science, language, and art? Does he mean to thrust salvation suddenly sidewise into our days, while we pursue everything but the soul's good throughout our life? No, let religion be an inspiration and continual culture too!

Single cases of failure in this attempt must not discredit the truth of general procedure.

Intervening obstructions in the line of all accomplishment disappoint sometimes the best hopes. So the children of the pious, of those most anxious for the sanctity of their offspring, — perhaps by some strange reaction of Nature seeking for herself a balance against a mistaken over-severity of austere requirements, — have been known to be irreligious and profane. The soul, especially as yet asleep in the child, is a peculiarly obscure region of observation. Lenses, that reach the finest molecule or farthest star, cannot penetrate it. Crucibles, that detect the poisonous particle, and make a link in the otherwise broken chain of evidence, cannot analyze the commencement of moral evil. But the great verdict of history is, that character and disposition go down, by an hereditary law as well as a special influence of fidelity, from parent to child. It is often asked, how soon education may begin. I answer, as soon as you can get an educator. That is what we want, — parents, guardians, teachers, that are educators. Be or have an educator, and infants in their cradles will be educated. Throw not the soul of your child out on the barren moor, to find sustenance for itself. Leave not your child until after he is grown up, then to judge independently, and altogether for himself, about religion. It is not, according to our cant, his right from you, but your wrong to him, that you should leave him without religious influence and prepossession. Prejudice him in favor of truth and virtue; as Coleridge told a friend, who was very anxious that the young should not be prejudiced in religion, that for his part he thought it would have been better if, instead of leaving his garden to weeds, growing of their own accord, he had prejudiced it a little in favor of roses and strawberries. Ah! we do and must prejudice our children to evil or good. What means the sob of grief I have seen pass direct from a mother's breast to her child's, — the one bosom beating exact time, like a pendulum, to the other, — but the natural and spiritual transmissibleness of all qualities? Into the first year of the new-comer crowd of themselves all the years of the progenitor. Shall we not voluntarily, with our utmost industry, avail ourselves of the power of this principle? Shall the space of the Church, unlike that of orchard and field, have no nursery? Shall the sailor's boy grow up to know every rope in the ship, and be haunted day and night by the sea; the artisan's child have cunning in his fingers, that itch for the tools from his birth; the sons of merchants, physicians, and counsellors feel the genius of the professions they so often follow in their after-career; and shall the seed of Christian parents show no flower of Divine grace or fruit of good living? Whatever we may say, a true ecclesiastical organization will appear only when our forms are luminous with our life. Else, they will have no more unction than there is of oil or flame in the rusty lamp from Pompeii, which you hang for a curiosity on your wall. Ordinances will serve us, when our own hearts feel and ever anew sustain and build them, as the shell-fish does the crystalline enamelled walls which are his forms, cemented in all their grains from his own substance; else, in either case, they are but unholy refuse. Holy-water, robes of white and gold, fragrant censers, choir and wafer, all the appeals of Rome to all the senses, are good only as they touch the soul. Whatever may be our outward modes, let their virtue be tried by all who will. Some pictures in foreign churches are covered with a veil, and exhibited only to those who can pay. So much the worse for the pictures. If the Church restrict its privileges, so much the worse for the organization of the Church,—so much the worse for the human soul!

CHAPTER XXI.

PROPORTION.

We read that, when Solomon was finishing the interior of his great building, he graved on the bases or tables, cherubim, lions, and palm-trees, according to the proportion or proper size of every one. What was the reason of such an engraving in the house of God? We can understand that the king should seek the crowning grace of proportion in the temple he was raising to the Divine worship and glory. He had an eye to see the same grace in all the world, so perfect that the Greeks called the universe Order or Beauty, though Ecclesiastes, the old Hebrew preacher, noticed as well as they, the same fact. Therefore it was not strange that, in the grand plan and every minute subdivision of his structure, even on the open space of a brazen table, Solomon should have every line wrought in exact proportion. But why were lions and palm-trees, as well as cherubim, engraven? How was a true proportion for the place in such things kept? The certain limited space he had, why did he thus fill? Nay, wherefore in a sanctuary were introduced manifold other designs, of the olive and pomegranate, open flowers and lily-work, living creatures and a molten sea? What propriety or significance had these common and secular objects? What sort of proportion verily could they add to a sacred edifice? Did this bringing into a shrine of prayer of all these earthly shapes, of trees of the wood, blossoms of the garden, beasts of the field, leaves of the forest, and watery waves, add pictures and associations that could start or further the transports of homage from the human bosom to the majesty of the Most High? Was not the monarch thinking of his own vanity, as well as the Divine honor? The drawing of the cherubim indeed, that spoke of invisible might and purity, was well enough, a substantial aid to prayer and communion with the Lord. But wherefore be at the pains to sketch, or indeed allow to be introduced, such outside, profane objects as lions and palms?

Such representations of natural grace and animal strength would not indeed to some chambers have been unsuited. They might have answered for the city hall, if they had one, in Jerusalem, or for the exchange and market-place, where we learn some traded and others sat idle, or for the place of gay worldly festivity. But how could they be appropriate within the walls and on the holy vessels of those dedicated courts? Why was not the entire amplitude of that room rather occupied and covered all over with a different kind of paintings, of nothing but angels, and sculptures of heavenly things, and symbols, in silver and gold, of a miraculous providence, every one of which would portray some supernatural interposition or celestial reality, and touch the heart to aspirations of wonder and thanksgiving? Many a cherub indeed, that marvellous type at whose explanation commentators have been so puzzled, yet whose four faces and wings, to look and move and fly every way, seem at least to shadow forth all-seeing and omnipresent attributes, was put in. But the question still confronts us, why was the artist's chisel employed to cut in the solid metal, for the respect of the Jews in their very adorations, animals and plants and terrestrial scenery also?

Truly deeper than the bronze surfaces, where the lines were imprinted, and most instructive still, is the meaning of the obvious, yet grand and irresistible reply. Because all these growths and creatures were the work of God, belonged to that creation the whole of which he called good, illustrated the richness and variety of his wisdom and love, and so were not only legitimate, but necessary to mark that proportion, of everything he ordains, which should be in our religion also, and alone can infuse health into the thoughts and feelings of the holiest hour; religion being truly no unnatural, technical, and confined thing, but wide as the world. So it is from no antiquarian, scholarly curiosity about that celebrated pile at Jerusalem, so long since torn down, that I have thus carefully described its style. I would only take from it the idea, — most timely, is it not? at this present moment, to correct our own aberrations and disorders, — that the same religious proportion which was expressed in its precious substances and exquisitely fashioned materials, should with a greater, inasmuch as a living beauty, be portrayed in our worship and our lives.

This virtue of moral proportion, though so often slighted, I think we can all appreciate. Nothing so much offends certainly any fair and delicate mind, as seeing anything out of proportion. It can scarce endure a door ajar, the hanging of a curtain awry, the awkward position of a utensil, or clumsy placing of a chair. Straightway it is eager to rectify the trivial mistake and offence. But, beneath all form and color, sound and pressure upon the senses of outward things, there is another and greater proportion, that penetrates into and vitally concerns the mind. Hence the advice in Shakespeare, great moralist as well as poet, which we all might take to heart, though volunteered only by an imaginary counsellor in the play to an imaginary traveller, to give no "unproportioned thought his act." Everybody speaks of the calmness of Jesus, the serenity in him, scarce for a moment ever perturbed. Whence did it arise, but from this complete inward proportion of his character, which all his disciples should copy? Let us not be excessive in any of our passions, expressions, or doings. To let ourselves go beyond the mark of conscience and truth is very soon to have madness in our mind, fire on our tongue, intemperance in our indulgences, and folly in our deeds. Neither let us come short in our love and duty to God and man; for that is want of proportion, well-nigh as bad on one side as disproportion is on the other.

In every relation we bear, every matter in which we are engaged, let nothing with us be what is vulgarly called *a rage*, but all in keeping, as after the divine proportion we strive. But, in concluding with this theme my essay, I have a special direction of treatment in view. That Almighty Maker, who fixed the order and proportion of day and night, promulgated to his most ancient people a memorable allotment, only in our times of battle or bloody revolution set aside, and which has proved its everlasting adaptation to our nature, of six days for labor, and the seventh for rest. This is but a single instance of what we proverbially say, — there is reason, that is proportion, in all things. One great and most momentous inquiry, therefore, suggested by that famous fourth commandment to hallow the Sabbath day, respects the proportion which all the forms of religion, of which particularly I have said so much, should have to the business of life. With all the reverence of religious people for the Scripture, Old Testament and New, inclining them to follow every way its hints, need I remark the fact so evident, that this proportion is not yet gained? By too little at one time, and too much at another, rather is it continually violated or departed from.

I do not, of course, mean to say the Bible for our pious public exercises would severely shut us up to a precise and mathematically measured seventh part of the time. But it doubtless does mean to hint a certain wholesome general, yet very large, something like a sixfold, proportion of active care and labor to contemplative prayer and rest. It certainly is very jealous, and in no words so much as in those uttered by Christ himself, of frequent ritual displays of the religious sentiment. All reason, all observation of human life, confirms herein its wisdom. If the Atlantic steamer, instead of keeping her hot force at her heart, hugging it to throb unseen, and through billow and tempest push her across the deep, were to display it in a flag of fire, she would not get along over the trackless waste at all. Neither shall we over the ocean of life heavenward, if we display our religion. Our Master does not teach us it is not well to be socially grateful, and pay together unto God our vows. But he does teach us it is better for the most part to signify our real religion in our ordinary daily course. He does teach us not to draw off by itself the mighty element of our devout feeling. He would not have us look at it as a mirror in which to admire ourselves. He does not exhort us to kindle our hearts to rapture with the flame of what is so fiery after its kind. Rather would he have us mix it in pure and blessed proportions with all our speech and conduct, and let it, according to his beautiful parable, as leaven in the meal, — not having the meal in one place and the leaven in another, — work through the whole mass and circuit of our earthly affairs and connections with mankind.

But is it not a more purely spiritual thing to pour out, in prayer and joyful rapture of the breast, the sensibilities that yearn after God, than it is to toil in the hard matter, and trudge in the muddy ways of this world? It may be so. Yes, more purely spiritual it may be. But pure spirituality is not the only thing we want for the perfection of our nature. God has put us into a work-shop. The sky is its roof indeed, for us to look at, "fretted" as it is "with golden fires." But the earth is its floor. These hands and faculties are its tools. As the lion and the palm were graven with the cherubim on Solomon's sacred tables, so we want strength and beauty, as well as spirituality, to complete our proper human excellence, and without the strength and beauty the spirituality itself will slip through our fingers, and in mere formality be speedily lost.

But wherefore have I adduced all these considerations now? To point a needful criticism, that may make us beware of a peril in our own times and land. Not that I would quarrel with our age or lot. I do not agree with those who think the world is growing, not better, but worse. Yet mankind, and in no country more than our own, is still exposed to this particular charge, of religious disproportion or deformity in the posture and action of its entire mental frame. I think no truer word has been spoken than lately, by the public lecturer on the general science of health, that what we want above all things is "a steadier movement in our American brain." Indeed, what doctor's authority or wise keeper of lunatics is needed to tell us we are all a little insane? It is an insane atmosphere we breathe. It affects us all somewhat. One case of derangement lately quelled the religious spasm of a whole town. But what numbers are partially deranged, often indeed about far other matters than religion!

A year ago, all was hot haste of pecuniary speculation. It seemed true, as eloquent speakers said, that the business of this generation was, according to the primeval decree, to subdue the earth and possess it. Cloisters and peaceful meditations and pious exercises, said our strong men, — O, all such things belong to the Middle Ages! Let us leave them there in the dark. Progress, forward in material prosperity, is our watchword. He shall be our captain who speaks in the most rousing tone, proposes the boldest adventure, and marches with the longest stride. The railroad and locomotive shall be printed for our pictorial motto, a type in everything of our railroad speed, as we call it, to luxury and wealth. All Europe was but our shop over the way, across the street or ferry, where, like a thriftless housekeeper, we were running up by the hundred million a tremendous account. At every spot that promised any return for trade and enterprise, in every wilderness after the sweet honey of gain, swarmed our twenty millions of people, like bees. Mines and mills, water-passages and land-passages, were opened or projected, in anticipation of a future century's real seasonableness, as if we could hurry, not ourselves only, but God. Lavish expenditure outstripped even fancied accumulation of earthly goods, till the freshet of wrath, laid up against the day of wrath, over all dams and bridges we thought might hold and span it, suddenly broke.

In what a state of disappointment, poverty, emptiness, and languor, as the devouring plague passed by, we were left! What should we do? Nature abhors a vacuum. It will not stay in a recoil. If we had only been possessed of the means, we should no doubt have rushed into pleasure, amusement, recreation, gay and overflowing parties without end, and perhaps the miserable feeding and stimulus of sensual appetites, released as we were so largely from the sobriety of regular tasks. Thank God that he made us so poor we had not the means, and thank him that there was something else, always indeed at the door of home and heart and public shrine, an inexpensive resource, which even the poor can have without money and without price, — even Religion! So at last, as other sublunary shapes of things, so ardently chased, vanish from our pursuit, we wake up to find that we had forgotten the cherubim. Now we seek the overshadowing glory they set forth. Witness the great revivals of religion, spreading through the country, far as the former panic and in the same quarters, agitating the great neighboring metropolis of the continent, and beginning to stir the interest of our own town!

How shall we regard it? Rejoice at it shall we not? Encourage and speed it shall we not? Attach ourselves to its motion and take seats in this lightning-train to heaven! Seek to be among those borne up on the fourfold wings of the cherubim! Yes, simply, purely, and altogether so, if there were the cherubim only for us to regard. Then we might fly off from this dull, dusty spot of heavy anxieties habitual and responsibilities. But in the engraving on the holy tables of Solomon in the temple of the Lord were the lion and the palm, as well as the cherubim, — strength and beauty, as well as spirituality. We human creatures do not look so handsome when we are flying off in mere transport and ecstasy, as when we show a gracious courtesy to

science, and the joyful mood, together in that state which the voice of inspiration so sublimely calls peace.

Herein would be a revival for ever; for this would be proportion. In such temperance and moderation would consist also the perfection and perpetual enthusiasm of our whole nature. Then we should be the same — patient, obedient, loving, and pure — everywhere, as Jesus was. Who, that saw him, did not see him the same, whether in street, house, temple, or synagogue? How much better if religion had been mingled with our affairs in the past, to prevent the crazy avarice, spendthrift scheming, and foolish finance, that have just had such a fall, the whole earth yet smokes and rings with the crash and the overthrow! How much better to instil it into all our activity in time to come, than to separate it, feebly cast ourselves into the tide of emotion, curse this world of God as evil, and reckon every industrial operation or success as naught, till, in the turn of the wheel, business shall become all in all once more, and religion cold and dead, — ay, and the very same persons now converted, apostate and needing to be converted again! Such is not His arithmetic. So Heaven calculates not the sum. The best saint is the holy man in the city street, not the holy man untempted in a cave.

If we never waked to a sense of our obligations to God, better that a tempest of religious excitement should wake us, than that we should sleep the sleep of death. But there is something more to do than to wake. We have got to work also, as well as rub our eyes. It is a good thing to establish our principles in social communion and meditation, but a better to apply them in life. It is a good thing to build the Leviathan, but a better to launch and send her on her voyage. The most charitable person is not he who tells of his fine feelings of compassion for the needy, but he that through the week is busy in their behalf. The most religious person is the man not most on his knees, but most on his feet in the righteous way. The most honest man is not the smooth promiser, nor even the growling paymaster, but the cheerfully just. "Is not my dollar good as his?" said one merchant to another.

now converted, apostate and needing to be converted again! Such is not His arithmetic. So Heaven calculates not the sum. The best saint is the holy man in the city street, not the holy man untempted in a cave.

If we never waked to a sense of our obligations to God, better that a tempest of religious excitement should wake us, than that we should sleep the sleep of death. But there is something more to do than to wake. We have got to work also, as well as rub our eyes. It is a good thing to establish our principles in social communion and meditation, but a better to apply them in life. It is a good thing to build the Leviathan, but a better to launch and send her on her voyage. The most charitable person is not he who tells of his fine feelings of compassion for the needy, but he that through the week is busy in their behalf. The most religious person is the man not most on his knees, but most on his feet in the righteous way. The most honest man is not the smooth promiser, nor even the growling paymaster, but the cheerfully just. "Is not my dollar good as his?" said one merchant to another.

"No," was the answer, "unless it goes with as good a disposition!" Let us engrave the signals of the old temple, then, on our modern shield. Let the cherubim with unearthly purity overshadow us. Let beauty, like the palm, grow up beside us. Let there be no lion in the way, but our heart the lion courageous against all sin. Then we shall at last be able to present our escutcheon to God.

THE END.

Boston, 135 Washington Street.
March, 1858.

NEW BOOKS AND NEW EDITIONS

PUBLISHED BY

TICKNOR AND FIELDS.

SIR WALTER SCOTT.

HOUSEHOLD EDITION OF THE WAVERLEY NOVELS. Price 75 cents a volume.

THOMAS DE QUINCEY.

CONFESSIONS OF AN ENGLISH OPIUM-EATER, AND SUSPIRIA DE PROFUNDIS. With Portrait. Price 75 cents.
BIOGRAPHICAL ESSAYS. Price 75 cents.
MISCELLANEOUS ESSAYS. Price 75 cents.
THE CÆSARS. Price 75 cents.
LITERARY REMINISCENCES. 2 vols. Price $1.50.
NARRATIVE AND MISCELLANEOUS PAPERS. 2 vols. Price $1.50.
ESSAYS ON THE POETS, &c. 1 vol. 16mo. Price 75 cents.
HISTORICAL AND CRITICAL ESSAYS. 2 vols. $1.50.
AUTOBIOGRAPHIC SKETCHES. 1 vol. Price 75 cents.
ESSAYS ON PHILOSOPHICAL WRITERS, &c. 2 vols. 16mo. Price $1.50.
LETTERS TO A YOUNG MAN, and other Papers. 1 vol. Price 75 cents.
THEOLOGICAL ESSAYS AND OTHER PAPERS. 2 vols. Price $1.50.
THE NOTE BOOK. 1 vol. Price 75 cents.
MEMORIALS AND OTHER PAPERS. 2 vols. 16mo. $1.50.

CHARLES READE.

PEG WOFFINGTON. A Novel. Price 75 cents.
CHRISTIE JOHNSTONE. A Novel. Price 75 cents.
CLOUDS AND SUNSHINE. A Novel. Price 75 cents.
'NEVER TOO LATE TO MEND.' 2 vols. Price $1.50.
WHITE LIES. A Novel. 1 vol. Price $1.00.
PROPRIA QUÆ MARIBUS and THE BOX TUNNEL. Price 25 cents.

WILLIAM HOWITT.

LAND, LABOR, AND GOLD. 2 vols. Price $2.00.
A BOY'S ADVENTURES IN AUSTRALIA. Price 75 cents.

HENRY W. LONGFELLOW.

POCKET EDITION OF POETICAL WORKS COMPLETE. two volumes. $1.75.

POCKET EDITION OF PROSE WORKS COMPLETE. In t volumes. $1.75.

THE SONG OF HIAWATHA. Price $1.00.

THE GOLDEN LEGEND. A Poem. Price $1.00.

POETICAL WORKS. This edition contains the six volumes m tioned below. In two volumes. 16mo. Boards, $2.00.

In separate Volumes, each 75 cents.

Voices of the Night.
Ballads and other Poems.
Spanish Student; a Play in Three Acts.
Belfry of Bruges, and other Poems.
Evangeline; a Tale of Acadie.
The Seaside and the Fireside.
The Waif. A Collection of Poems. Edited by Longfellow.
The Estray. A Collection of Poems. Edited by Longfellow.

MR. LONGFELLOW'S PROSE WORKS.

HYPERION. A Romance. Price $1.00.
OUTRE-MER. A Pilgrimage. Price $1.00.
KAVANAGH. A Tale. Price 75 cents.

Illustrated editions of Evangeline, Poems, Hyperion, and ' Golden Legend.

ALFRED TENNYSON.

POETICAL WORKS. With Portrait. 2 vols. Cloth. $2.00.
THE PRINCESS. Cloth. Price 50 cents.
IN MEMORIAM. Cloth. Price 75 cents.
MAUD, and other Poems. Cloth. Price 50 cents.
POCKET EDITION OF POEMS COMPLETE. Price 75 cts.

OLIVER WENDELL HOLMES.

POEMS. With fine Portrait. Boards. $1.00. Cloth. $1.12.
ASTRÆA. Fancy paper. Price 25 cents.

NATHANIEL HAWTHORNE.

TWICE-TOLD TALES. Two volumes. Price $1.50.

THE SCARLET LETTER. Price 75 cents.

THE HOUSE OF THE SEVEN GABLES. Price $1.00.

THE SNOW IMAGE, AND OTHER TWICE-TOLD TALES. Price 75 cents.

THE BLITHEDALE ROMANCE. Price 75 cents.

MOSSES FROM AN OLD MANSE. New Edition. 2 vols. Price $1.50.

TRUE STORIES FROM HISTORY AND BIOGRAPHY. With four fine Engravings. Price 75 cents.

A WONDER-BOOK FOR GIRLS AND BOYS. With seven fine Engravings. Price 75 cents.

TANGLEWOOD TALES. Another 'Wonder-Book.' With Engravings. Price 88 cents.

BARRY CORNWALL.

ENGLISH SONGS AND OTHER SMALL POEMS. Enlarged Edition. Price $1.00.

DRAMATIC POEMS. Just published. $1.00.

ESSAYS AND TALES IN PROSE. 2 vols. Price $1.50.

JAMES RUSSELL LOWELL.

COMPLETE POETICAL WORKS. In Blue and Gold. 2 vols. Price $1.50.

POETICAL WORKS. Revised, with Additions. Two volumes, 16mo. Cloth. Price $1.50.

SIR LAUNFAL. New Edition. Price 25 cents.

A FABLE FOR CRITICS. New Edition. Price 50 cents.

THE BIGLOW PAPERS. A New Edition. Price 63 cents.

COVENTRY PATMORE.

THE ANGEL IN THE HOUSE. BETROTHAL.

" " " " ESPOUSALS. Price 75 cents each.

CHARLES KINGSLEY.

TWO YEARS AGO. A New Novel. Price $1.25.
AMYAS LEIGH. A Novel. Price $1.25.
GLAUCUS; OR, THE WONDERS OF THE SHORE. 50 cents.
POETICAL WORKS. Price 75 cents.
THE HEROES; OR, GREEK FAIRY TALES. 75 cents.
A NEW VOLUME OF POEMS. (In Press.)
LECTURES, ESSAYS, AND MISCELLANEOUS WRITING (In Press.)

CHARLES SUMNER.

ORATIONS AND SPEECHES. 2 vols. $2.50.
RECENT SPEECHES AND ADDRESSES. $1.25.

JOHN G. WHITTIER.

POCKET EDITION OF POETICAL WORKS. 2 volumes. $1.5
OLD PORTRAITS AND MODERN SKETCHES. 75 cents.
MARGARET SMITH'S JOURNAL. Price 75 cents.
SONGS OF LABOR, AND OTHER POEMS. Boards. 50 cents
THE CHAPEL OF THE HERMITS. Cloth. 50 cents.
LITERARY RECREATIONS AND MISCELLANIES. Cloth. $1
THE PANORAMA, AND OTHER POEMS. Cloth. 50 Cents

ALEXANDER SMITH.

A LIFE DRAMA. 1 vol. 16mo. 50 cents.
CITY POEMS. 1 vol. 16mo. 63 cents.

EDWIN P. WHIPPLE.

ESSAYS AND REVIEWS. 2 vols. Price $2.00.
LECTURES ON SUBJECTS CONNECTED WITH LITERATURE AND LIFE. Price 63 cents.
WASHINGTON AND THE REVOLUTION. Price 20 cents.

GEORGE S. HILLARD.

SIX MONTHS IN ITALY. 1 vol. 16mo. Price $1.50.
DANGERS AND DUTIES OF THE MERCANTILE PROFESSION. Price 25 cents.
SELECTIONS FROM THE WRITINGS OF WALTER SAVAGE LANDOR. 1 vol. 16mo. Price 75 cents.

HENRY GILES.

LECTURES, ESSAYS, AND MISCELLANEOUS WRITINGS. 2 vols. Price $1.50.

DISCOURSES ON LIFE. Price 75 cents.

ILLUSTRATIONS OF GENIUS. Cloth. $1.00.

BAYARD TAYLOR.

POEMS OF HOME AND TRAVEL. Cloth. Price 75 cents.

POEMS OF THE ORIENT. Cloth. 75 cents.

WILLIAM MOTHERWELL.

POEMS, NARRATIVE AND LYRICAL. New Ed. $1.25.

POSTHUMOUS POEMS. Boards. Price 50 cents.

MINSTRELSY, ANC. AND MOD. 2 vols. Boards. $1.50.

ROBERT BROWNING.

POETICAL WORKS. 2 vols. $2.00.

MEN AND WOMEN. 1 vol. Price $1.00.

CAPT. MAYNE REID'S JUVENILE BOOKS.

THE PLANT HUNTERS. 1 vol. 16mo. Price 75 cents.

THE DESERT HOME: OR, THE ADVENTURES OF A LOST FAMILY IN THE WILDERNESS. With fine Plates, $1.00.

THE BOY HUNTERS. With fine Plates. Just published. Price 75 cents.

THE YOUNG VOYAGEURS: OR, THE BOY HUNTERS IN THE NORTH. With Plates. Price 75 cents.

THE FOREST EXILES. With fine Plates. 75 cents.

THE BUSH BOYS. With fine Plates. 75 cents.

THE YOUNG YÄGERS. With fine Plates. 75 cents.

RAN AWAY TO SEA: AN AUTOBIOGRAPHY FOR BOYS. With fine Plates. 75 cents.

a *

GOETHE'S WRITINGS.

WILHELM MEISTER. Translated by THOMAS CARLYLE. 2 vo
Price $2.50.
FAUST. Translated by HAYWARD. Price 75 cents.
FAUST. Translated by CHARLES T. BROOKS. Price $1.00.

R. H. STODDARD.

POEMS. Cloth. Price 63 cents.
ADVENTURES IN FAIRY LAND. Price 75 cents.
SONGS OF SUMMER. Price 75 cents.

REV. CHARLES LOWELL, D. D

PRACTICAL SERMONS. 1 vol. 12mo. $1.25.
OCCASIONAL SERMONS. With fine Portrait. $1.25.

GEORGE LUNT.

LYRIC POEMS, &c. Cloth. 63 cents.
JULIA. A Poem. 50 cents.

PHILIP JAMES BAILEY.

THE MYSTIC, AND OTHER POEMS. 50 cents.
THE ANGEL WORLD, &c. 50 cents.

ANNA MARY HOWITT.

AN ART STUDENT IN MUNICH. Price $1.25.
A SCHOOL OF LIFE. A Story. Price 75 cents.

MRS. JAMESON.

CHARACTERISTICS OF WOMEN. Blue and gold. 75 cents
LOVES OF THE POETS. " " 75 cents
DIARY OF AN ENNUYÉE. " " 75 cents
SKETCHES OF ART, &c. " " 75 cents

MARY RUSSELL MITFORD.

OUR VILLAGE. Illustrated. 2 vols. 16mo. Price $2.50.
ATHERTON, AND OTHER STORIES. 1 vol. 16mo. $1.25.

MRS. CROSLAND.

LYDIA: A WOMAN'S BOOK. Cloth. Price 75 cents.
ENGLISH TALES AND SKETCHES. Cloth. $1.00.
MEMORABLE WOMEN. Illustrated. $1.00.

GRACE GREENWOOD.

GREENWOOD LEAVES. 1st & 2d Series. $1.25 each.

POETICAL WORKS. With fine Portrait. Price 75 cents.

HISTORY OF MY PETS. With six fine Engravings. Scarlet cloth. Price 50 cents.

RECOLLECTIONS OF MY CHILDHOOD. With six fine Engravings. Scarlet cloth. Price 50 cents.

HAPS AND MISHAPS OF A TOUR IN EUROPE. Price $1.25.

MERRIE ENGLAND. A new Juvenile. Price 75 cents.

A FOREST TRAGEDY, AND OTHER TALES. $1.00.

STORIES AND LEGENDS. A new Juvenile. Price 75 cents.

MRS. MOWATT.

AUTOBIOGRAPHY OF AN ACTRESS. Price $1.25.
PLAYS. ARMAND AND FASHION. Price 50 cents.
MIMIC LIFE. 1 vol. Price $1.25.
THE TWIN ROSES. 1 vol. Price 75 cents.

MRS. HOWE.

PASSION FLOWERS. Price 75 cents.
WORDS FOR THE HOUR. Price 75 cents.
THE WORLD'S OWN. Price 50 cents.

JOSIAH PHILLIPS QUINCY.

LYTERIA: A DRAMATIC POEM. Price 50 cents.
CHARICLES: A DRAMATIC POEM. Price 50 cents.

ALICE CARY.

POEMS. 1 vol. 16mo. Price $1.00.
CLOVERNOOK CHILDREN. With Plates. 75 cents.

MRS. ELIZA B. LEE.

MEMOIR OF THE BUCKMINSTERS. $1.25.
FLORENCE, THE PARISH ORPHAN. 50 cents.
PARTHENIA. 1 vol. 16mo. Price $1.00.

MRS. JUDSON.

ALDERBROOK. BY FANNY FORRESTER. 2 vols. Price $1.7
THE KATHAYAN SLAVE, AND OTHER PAPERS. 1 v. Price 63 cents.
MY TWO SISTERS: A SKETCH FROM MEMORY. Price 50 cen

POETRY.

LEIGH HUNT'S POEMS. Blue and gold. 2 vols. $1.50.
GERALD MASSEY'S POETICAL WORKS. Blue and go 75 cents.
W. M. THACKERAY. BALLADS. 1 vol. 16mo. 75 cents.
CHARLES MACKAY'S POEMS. 1 vol. Cloth. Price $1.00.
HENRY ALFORD'S POEMS. Just out. Price $1.25.
RICHARD MONCKTON MILNES. POEMS OF MANY YEA Boards. Price 75 cents.
GEORGE H. BOKER. PLAYS AND POEMS. 2 vols. Price $2.0
CHARLES SPRAGUE. POETICAL AND PROSE WRITINGS. Wi fine Portrait. Boards. Price 75 cents.
GERMAN LYRICS. Translated by CHARLES T. BROOKS. 1 v 16mo. Cloth. Price $1.00.
MATTHEW ARNOLD'S POEMS. Price 75 cents.
W. EDMONSTOUNE AYTOUN. BOTHWELL. Price 75 cents.

THOMAS W. PARSONS. POEMS. Price $1.00.

JOHN G. SAXE. POEMS. With Portrait. Boards, 63 cents. Cloth, 75 cents.

HENRY T. TUCKERMAN. POEMS. Cloth. Price 75 cents.

BOWRING'S MATINS AND VESPERS. Price 50 cents.

YRIARTE'S FABLES. Translated by G. H. DEVEREUX. Price 63 cents.

MEMORY AND HOPE. A BOOK OF POEMS, REFERRING TO CHILDHOOD. Cloth. Price $2.00.

THALATTA: A BOOK FOR THE SEA-SIDE. 1 vol. 16mo. Cloth. Price 75 cents.

PHŒBE CARY. POEMS AND PARODIES. 75 cents.

PREMICES. By E. FOXTON. Price $1.00.

PAUL H. HAYNE. Poems. 1 vol. 16mo. 63 cents.

PERCIVAL'S POEMS. Blue and Gold. (In Press.)

MISCELLANEOUS.

G. H. LEWES. THE LIFE AND WORKS OF GOETHE. 2 vols. 16mo. $2.50.

OAKFIELD. A Novel. By LIEUT. ARNOLD. Price $1.00.

ESSAYS ON THE FORMATION OF OPINIONS AND THE PURSUIT OF TRUTH. 1 vol. 16mo. Price $1.00.

WALDEN: OR, LIFE IN THE WOODS. By HENRY D. THOREAU. 1 vol. 16mo. Price $1.00.

LIGHT ON THE DARK RIVER: OR, MEMOIRS OF MRS. HAMLIN. 1 vol. 16mo. Cloth. Price $1.00.

WASHINGTON ALLSTON. MONALDI, a Tale. 1 vol. 16mo. 75 cents.

PROFESSOR E. T. CHANNING. LECTURES ON ORATORY AND RHETORIC. Price 75 cents.

JOHN C. FREMONT. LIFE, EXPLORATIONS, &c. With Illustrations. Price 75 cents.

SEED-GRAIN FOR THOUGHT AND DISCUSSION. Compiled by MRS. A. C. LOWELL. 2 vols. $1.75.

A PHYSICIAN'S VACATION. By DR. WALTER CHANNING Price $1.50.

MRS. HORACE MANN. A PHYSIOLOGICAL COOKERY BOOK. 63c

ROBERTSON'S SERMONS. 1 vol. 12mo. $1.00.

SCHOOL DAYS AT RUGBY. By AN OLD BOY. 1 vol. 16 Price $1.00.

WILLIAM MOUNTFORD. THORPE: A QUIET ENGLISH TOW AND HUMAN LIFE THEREIN. 16mo. Price $1.00.

NOTES FROM LIFE. BY HENRY TAYLOR, author of 'Phi Van Artevelde.' 1 vol. 16mo. Cloth. Price 63 cents.

REJECTED ADDRESSES. By HORACE and JAMES SMI Boards, Price 50 cents. Cloth, 63 cents.

WARRENIANA. A Companion to the 'Rejected Addresses.' Pr 63 cents.

WILLIAM WORDSWORTH'S BIOGRAPHY. 2 vols. $2.50.

ART OF PROLONGING LIFE. By HUFELAND. Edited ERASMUS WILSON, F. R. S. 1 vol. 16mo. Price 75 cents.

JOSEPH T. BUCKINGHAM'S PERSONAL MEMOIRS A RECOLLECTIONS OF EDITORIAL LIFE. With Portr 2 vols. 16mo. Price $1.50.

VILLAGE LIFE IN EGYPT. By the Author of 'Purple Tints Paris.' 2 vols. 16mo. Price $1.25.

DR. JOHN C. WARREN. THE PRESERVATION OF HEALTH, 1 vol. Price 38 cents.

PRIOR'S LIFE OF EDMUND BURKE. 2 vols. $2.00.

NATURE IN DISEASE. BY DR. JACOB BIGELOW. 1 vol. 16 Price $1.25.

WENSLEY: A STORY WITHOUT A MORAL. Price 75 cents.

GOLDSMITH. THE VICAR OF WAKEFIELD. Illustrated Editi Price $3.00.

PALISSY THE POTTER. By the Author of 'How to make Ho Unhealthy.' 2 vols. 16mo. Price $1.50.

THE BARCLAYS OF BOSTON. By Mrs. H. G. Otis. 1 vol. 12mo. $1.25.

HORACE MANN. Thoughts for a Young Man. 25 cents.

F. W. P. GREENWOOD. Sermons of Consolation $1.00.

THE BOSTON BOOK. Price $1.25.

ANGEL-VOICES. Price 38 cents.

SIR ROGER DE COVERLEY. From the 'Spectator.' 75 cents.

S. T. WALLIS. Spain, her Institutions, Politics, and Public Men. Price $1.00.

MEMOIR OF ROBERT WHEATON. 1 vol. Price $1.00.

LABOR AND LOVE: A Tale of English Life. 50 cents.

Mrs. PUTNAM'S RECEIPT BOOK; An Assistant to Housekeepers. 1 vol. 16mo. Price 50 cents.

Mrs. A. C. LOWELL. Education of Girls. Price 25 cents.

THE SOLITARY OF JUAN FERNANDEZ. By the Author of Picciola. Price 50 cents.

RUTH. A New Novel by the Author of 'Mary Barton.' Cheap Edition. Price 38 cents.

EACH OF THE ABOVE POEMS AND PROSE WRITINGS, MAY BE HAD IN VARIOUS STYLES OF HANDSOME BINDING.

☞ Any book published by Ticknor & Fields, will be sent by mail, postage free, on receipt of publication price.

Their stock of Miscellaneous Books is very complete, and they respectfully solicit orders from CITY AND COUNTRY LIBRARIES.

ILLUSTRATED

JUVENILE BOOKS.

CURIOUS STORIES ABOUT FARIES. 75 cents.
KIT BAM'S ADVENTURES. 75 cents.
THE FOREST EXILES. 75 cents.
THE DESERT HOME. $1.00.
THE BOY HUNTERS. 75 cents.
THE YOUNG VOYAGEURS. 75 cents.
THE BUSH BOYS. 75 cents.
THE YOUNG YÄGERS. 75 cents.
THE PLANT HUNTERS. 75 cents.
RAN AWAY TO SEA. 75 cents.
A BOY'S ADVENTURES IN AUSTRALIA. 75 cents.
RAINBOWS FOR CHILDREN. 75 cents.
THE MAGICIAN'S SHOW BOX. 75 cents.
TANGLEWOOD TALES. 75 cents.
A WONDER BOOK FOR GIRLS AND BOYS. 75 cents.
TRUE STORIES FROM HISTORY AND BIOGRAPHY. 75 c
MERRIE ENGLAND. By Grace Greenwood. 75 cents.
STORIES AND LEGENDS. 75 cents.
CLOVERNOOK CHILDREN. 75 cents.
ADVENTURES IN FAIRY LAND. 75 cents.
HISTORY OF MY PETS. By Grace Greenwood. 50 cents.
RECOLLECTIONS OF MY CHILDHOOD. 50 cents.
OUR GRANDMOTHER'S STORIES. 50 cents.
FLORENCE, THE PARISH ORPHAN. 50 cents.
MEMOIRS OF A LONDON DOLL. 50 cents.
THE DOLL AND HER FRIENDS. 50 cents.
TALES FROM CATLAND. 50 cents.
AUNT EFFIE'S RHYMES FOR LITTLE CHILDREN. 75 cen
THE STORY OF AN APPLE. 50 cents.
THE GOOD-NATURED BEAR. 75 cents.
PETER PARLEY'S SHORT STORIES FOR LONG NIGHT 50 cents.
THE HISTORY OF THE AMERICAN REVOLUTION. 38 cen
THE HISTORY OF THE NEW ENGLAND STATES. 38 cen
THE HISTORY OF THE MIDDLE STATES. 38 cents.
THE HISTORY OF THE SOUTHERN STATES. 38 cents.
THE HISTORY OF THE WESTERN STATES. 38 cents.
THE SOLITARY OF JUAN FERNANDEZ. 50 cents.
JACK HALLIARD'S VOYAGES. 38 cents.
THE INDESTRUCTIBLE BOOKS FOR CHILDREN. Each cents.

www.ingramcontent.com/pod-product-compliance
Lightning Source LLC
LaVergne TN
LVHW010134110826
845151LV00002B/353

* 9 7 8 1 4 2 5 5 3 9 1 4 6 *